THE DUAL IMAGE

THE DUAL IMAGE

The Figure of the Jew

in

English and American Literature

by

HAROLD FISCH

KTAV PUBLISHING HOUSE, INC.

NEW YORK

THE DUAL IMAGE

by

Harold Fisch

INTRODUCTION

Coleridge remarked in his *Table-Talk* for August 14, 1833:

> The two images farthest removed from each other which can be comprehended under one term, are, I think, Isaiah— "Hear, O heavens, and give ear, O earth!"—and Levi of Holywell Street—"Old Clothes!"—both of them Jews, you'll observe.

This contradiction between the two images of the Jew as perceived by Coleridge may stand as a fitting opening text for this study. The Jew is seen as both noble and ignoble, black and white; from one angle he is a paragon, from another, he is a worm and no man. Different authors may see the contradictions in different terms, but they are always there, not only for the non-Jew, but for the Jewish writer also as he views himself through the prism of his self-awareness. The Jew is inevitably a figure of polarity, of radical ambiguity. Why should this be so? In this book, we shall be concerned with the literary evidence, but it is clear that the question has sociological, psychological and theological bearings also which cannot be entirely overlooked.

The literary portrayal of the Jew has now become a major theme for critics. James Joyce's *Ulysses* at the beginning of the modern period, and Saul Bellow's *Herzog* more recently, occupy the centre of attention as attempts to define the human predicament. In an age in which the characteristic literary mode is tragicomedy, the contradictions of Jewish existence, its climaxes and anti-climaxes, have become paradigms for a universal reality. But even if we look further back into the earlier periods of English and American literature, we find that the paradoxical image of the Jew is far from being (for the authors who treated it) a mere literary curiosity. Whether he appears as Saint or Devil, or both simultaneously, the Jew functions as a literary archetype. There is something compulsive about him: like the Ancient Mariner he demands attention. To chart this subject is to follow a major theme through Chaucer, Shakespeare, Milton, Sir Walter Scott, George Eliot, and other leading writers down to the present day.

The subject of the Jew in English and American literature is here treated "significantly rather than curiously." What is attempted is a broad survey of the subject with the more characteristic and important examples pinpointed, rather than a comprehensive history. This book first appeared in a shorter form in 1959 as a contribution to the Popular Jewish Library (Second Series). It has now been revised and enlarged. The last three chapters, dealing with recent American and British writing, are new.

Harold Fisch

Bar-Ilan University,
Israel.
1970

ACKNOWLEDGEMENTS

Acknowledgment is hereby made to the following for kind permission to quote copyright material: to Alfred A. Knopf Inc., for permission to quote from Abraham M. Klein's poem *The Second Scroll*; to Behrman House Inc., for permission to quote from Abraham M. Klein's *Hath Not a Jew* (1940); to Jonathan Cape Ltd., London, and to Random House, Inc. New York, for permission to quote passages from Nathaniel Tarn's *Old Savage/New City* (1964), and *The Beautiful Contradictions* (1969); to Random House Inc., New York, for permission to quote from Karl J. Shapiro's *Poems of a Jew* (1958), and to Mr. Emanuel Litvinoff for permission to quote from his poem on T. S. Eliot.

TABLE OF CONTENTS

CHAPTER ONE

THE MEDIEVAL PERIOD

Origins

The Jew is a personage of some importance both in the imagination of medieval man and in his daily affairs. As a financier, he provided the essential capital for industry and commerce: as unofficial tax-collector, he stood between the King and the nobility, supporting the latter in their building enterprises and channelling the profits into the Exchequer of the Jews for the benefit of the King. It is no accident that the period of his expulsion from England (1290) coincided with the decline of his material resources through taxation, and through arbitrary exactions and fines. His relation to the King was the epitome of his relation to medieval society as a whole. As a banker (then termed usurer) the Jew was utilized by all classes in a community still largely bound by primitive economics of barter: for his pains the Jew was reviled and persecuted, and when his usefulness was exhausted, he was banished. The nobleman treated him with a contempt he would not show to the lowest of his serfs.

In literature likewise, the Jew forces himself upon us everywhere, in ballads, in religious allegory, in drama, in sermons. He functions as a well-established and necessary myth, ubiquitous, coloured (in plays he wore red hair and a distinctive garb), unmistakable (as he was in daily life), declaring himself in grotesque gestures, stimulating in the reader or audience what, in literary criticism, is known as a " stock response." Literary critics sometimes consider " stock responses " as literary evils; only original percep-

11

tions based upon the writer's experience of the world matter. This point of view omits what one might term the ritual element in literature: literature as the vessel of public themes, conventions, and the myths of the human race, which the man of imagination—just because he is a man of imagination—makes articulate.

From this point of view, the figure of the Jew in literature, certainly in English literature, is an example of a myth of great power, functioning through stock responses and with the very minimum of reference to contemporary reality. We should remind ourselves that from 1290 to 1656, the period within which three of the greatest English poets, namely, Shakespeare, Marlowe, and Chaucer, turned their attention to Jews, there were no officially recognised Jews resident in the British Isles and available, as it were, for inspection. If we were to pursue this point along the lines of a psychological inquiry we might consider the Jew as a kind of Jungian archetype, issuing from the collective unconsciousness of medieval man. Indeed he does appear in close association with one unmistakable archetype of this kind, namely the Devil. But this would be to distort the picture more than a little, for the Jew is always more than a subjective psychological symbol: he is always, in however remote and perverted a way, the Jew of History, charged with having played a certain part in the death of the Christian saviour, carrying upon himself the burden of exile, and living (as he undoubtedly did) upon the profits of usury—alone, hated, hostile, itinerant, cherishing his own faith, guarding the ways and customs of his ancestors, and refusing " the summons to Christian fellowship."

Here then is a myth, which is at the same time an interpretation of history, and a distorting mirror held up to the life of a not insignificant component of medieval society. We may ask, what is the nature of the image produced? What kind of a figure is this Jew of the literary imagination? At this point, we must guard against first impressions, for the region of myth is also the region of mystery.

The Devil for instance is a complex figure in literature: for Byron, Blake, and Milton, the Christian Devil is the poet's hero. First impressions of Lucifer are nearly always wrong. The Jew is even more complicated because here the literary imagination is grapppling (as we have already said) with an *historical* problem, the problem of the survival of the Jew, of his inner spiritual integrity (or from the gentile point of view, his obstinacy), and of the maddening combination in the actual bearing of the Jew, of a sense of his own distinct superiority to the non-Jew, together with a humble (or from the gentile point of view, cringing) acceptance of the badge of shame, the branding-tool, and the bloody whip. The Jew is often (we might even say, most often) a figure of evil: but more than he is a figure of evil, he is a nuisance, a problem, a difficulty, something one has to come to terms with before one can come to terms with oneself.

The image of the Jew in literature is indeed a dual image: he excites horror, fear, hatred; but he also excites wonder, awe, and love. The literature about the Jew is a literature which attempts either to abolish one or other of these images, or somehow to bring the two into a common focus. This might be affirmed generally of the figure of the Jew in all literature, but in Western Christendom. the dual image of the Jew has behind it a well-formulated and distinct *theological* sanction, which serves to heighten and intensify the component parts of the image, to render them more disturbing for the Christian believer, for whom a proper attitude to the Jew becomes necessary in clarifying his own religious profession.

The central texts governing the Christian conception of the Jew and his place in the religious economy of mankind, are provided in the Epistles of Paul. He writes to the Galatians: "For as many as are of the works of the law are under the curse." Agobard and Chrysostom in the Middle Ages took the hint and pronounced the most violent maledictions upon the Jews and their doings. Such execration looks back too to the furious attacks by Stephen upon the men of the Synagogue (*Acts,* vi-vii), and to the evil picture of the Scribes and Pharisees afforded in the gospels. But as James Parkes has pointed out, Paul's relation to the old Israel was more dialectical than Chrysostom seemed to suppose; the New Testament generally presupposes the Old Testament, that is to say, Jewish covenant history and the tradition of the Prophets and the Patriarchs, as the warrant and ground of its own claims. But Paul goes further: he requires the contemporary Jew, the Jew of post-Biblical history as a witness to the final consummation of the Christian promise of salvation: or to put it a little more accurately, he requires the regeneration of Israel as the true source of regeneration for all mankind. This we may say is Hebrew doctrine likewise; but the difference for Paul is that the regeneration of Israel is accomplished *through his conversion to Christianity,* and by no other way. " God hath not cast away his people which he foreknew," Paul declares in his letter to the Romans. And he goes on with the famous image of Israel as the good olive tree, and the gentiles as the wild olive tree. He tells his hearers, "Thou being a wild olive tree wert graffed in among them, and with Boast not against the branches. But if thou boast thou them partakest of the root and fatness of the olive tree: bearest not the root, but the root thee . . . For if thou wert cut out of the olive tree which is wild by nature, and wert graffed contrary to nature into a good olive tree: how much more shall these, which be the natural branches, be graffed into their own olive tree?" (Ch. xi.) Such reintegration was an essential part of the Christian hope.

The Jew would survive to testify to the ultimate triumph of the divine plan of salvation, this plan being to Paul synonymous with the messiahship of Jesus. This dialectical attitude to the Jew explains the special status he "enjoyed" —if that is the right term—in the Middle Ages. He had to be kept outside the pale of society: but he also had to be preserved. Hence the legally sanctioned Jewry or Jews' Street, and later, the Ghetto; hence the special laws governing the existence and conduct of the Jewish community; hence the effort of the Papacy to protect the Jew from the mob and from the worst forms of calumny. The Jews were a deicide nation but they were also a nation which is redeemed, and on whose redemption the fate of mankind hangs. From this state of mind arises the two-fold image of the Jew in the Christian literature of the Middle Ages and beyond.

Mysteries and Miracles

Medieval plays and the medieval ballad had something of a European currency. The religious drama in which the Jew makes his most emphatic appearance began as an elaboration of the Latin Mass which of course had a standard form throughout Western Christendom—so that it is not surprising that the character of the Jew as depicted becomes an international rather than a national convention.

In the German *Benediktbeuern* series of Mystery plays, the chief Jewish character is *Archisynagogus,* and the actor is instructed to " imitate the gestures of a Jew in all things " (the Jew always being considered as given to extravagant gesticulation). Mary, in a speech of some bitterness, addresses the Jews as a " blind and lamentable people " and urges them to do penance before Jesus who will then forgive them for their stubbornness. The chief Jewish character in the gospel plays or Mysteries was Judas. His name was sufficient to identify him with the Jew in general (*Judaeus*); and he is depicted not merely as traitor but as an usurer as well! We may notice how curiously realism and mythology mingle in such examples. In England, the Cycle of Mystery Plays acted at York on Corpus Christi Day during the fourteenth and fifteenth centuries, gives us numerous examples of Judas in his composite character. These plays are no longer in Latin but in English and they have accordingly a more popular appeal and accent. Much is made of the conspiracy of

Judas and Pilate. Judas, like a bargaining usurer asks for thirty pence saying that he would like to " make a marchandise "; he grumbles when the Romans fail to hand the money over at once. He is also described as Christ's treasurer, in which office he had shown his " Jewish " instincts by converting ten per cent. of the money to his own use—a fact which receives special emphasis in the play.

It is obvious that in such an example the Jew is not merely odious but comical as well. Judas's red wig (later bequeathed to Shylock) becomes a semi-comic melodrama feature; also the grotesque gesticulations of the Jew in early literature (always insisted upon) serve to degrade the Jew in the eyes of the spectator: but they also serve to do something else: they ensure that the Jew is never taken too seriously. Perhaps this is part of the defensive structure of the myth; for if the Jew is taken seriously some of his odiousness will disappear, which in fact is what happens in Shakespeare's *Merchant of Venice*. That play breaks with the tradition in one important respect: from time to time Shylock becomes a tragic rather than a comic character.

But to return to the medieval scene, the impression should not be given that the Jew of the Mystery Plays is a pure figure of fun. If he inspired derision, he also inspired fear, the fear which is associated in the medieval imagination with the Devil. We should remember that in the gospel account, the betrayal by Judas is accomplished through the inspiration of Satan, and in collusion with the Jewish Priests and Pharisees (the fact that the other eleven apostles are also Jews receives no emphasis in the Middle Ages): " And the chief priests and scribes sought how they might kill him; for they feared the people. Then entered Satan into Judas surnamed Iscariot being of the number of the twelve. And he went his way, and communed with the chief priests and captains, how he might betray him unto them " (*Luke*, xxii). The triangle is complete: the Jews, Judas, and the Devil. Joshua Trachtenberg shows that in the Middle Ages, not merely are the Jews regarded as devilish, but the Devil himself becomes a Jew and is depicted as such on the stage—he too for instance has red hair and a long nose. In general, the connexion between the Devil and the Jews is part of the convention. Chaucer in the *Prioress's Tale* speaks of

> Our firste foo, the serpent Sathanas,
> That hath in Jewes hert his waspes nest.

and in *The Merchant of Venice,* Launcelot Gobbo describes his master as " the very Devil incarnal ". When Salanio sees Shylock coming (Act III, scene i), he says the Devil comes " in the likeness of a Jew ".

We may think that we now have a fairly clear idea of the Jew on the medieval stage. The characteristics of Judas are reproduced in the other supposedly typical Jews, as for instance Herod whose Edomite origin is conveniently ignored. Herod's bragging comes to be regarded as an important Jewish habit (note the expression " to outherod Herod "). Other Jewish characteristics are distributed between Caiaphas, Annas, and the Pharisees.

All this, however, represents only one side of the picture. In the Miracle plays based on the Old Testament we have something quite different—the Jew as hero: Noah the Patriarchs, Moses, Daniel, and the Prophets all make their appearance. And of course, three of the Nine Worthies of medieval legend (as Shakespeare was later to present them in the last act of *Love's Labour's Lost*) are Jews. In such cases, cringing changes to patience and long-suffering: stubbornness to constancy: the very differences of Jewish habit and dress which served to force the Devil-Jew upon the attention as a pariah, an outcast, or a figure of fun, now serve to distinguish the Children of Israel as the Chosen People, enjoying those covenant privileges and those distinctive laws which the Christian believer so much desired to inherit. Mostly Biblical Jewish figures are treated typologically, as symbols or presentments of Christian virtues, but something of their human substance

is retained. Nor should it be thought that, somehow, the
Children of Israel in the Old Testament plays were not
thought of as Jews. Certainly they were not so clearly
associated with the *contemporary* Jew as was Judas, but
the connexion was nevertheless unmistakable. In the Latin
Ordo de Ysaac et Rebecca, originating evidently in twelfth
century Austria, the stage directions indicate that Isaac
and his sons are to wear " pilea Judaica," i.e., Jewish
caps. In the sixteenth century English Interlude of *Jacob
and Esau* (possibly by Nicholas Udall), the title-page of
the quarto of 1568 announces, " The partes and names
of the Players who are to be considered to be Hebrews
and so should be apparailed with attire." Jacob the Jew
is, in this play, the saint; his brother Esau, the lewd ruffian.
The cunning which Rebecca persuades Jacob to practise
on his father is a " prety knacke " justified by its motives
and results: in the antisemitic plays such behaviour would
of course be castigated as foul deceit and knavery. This
will indicate the difference in emotional climate between
the two.

Old Testament plays were not as common in the Middle
Ages as were the Passion plays dwelling on the specifically
Christian hope, with their more negative portrayal of
the Jew. In the Reformation era, however, the balance is
reversed—Jesus and the apostles are rarely seen on the
stage: David and the Patriarchs remain. With the secularization of the Drama in the Renaissance era, the Old
Testament (unlike the New) is found to be a rich source
of dramatic episodes—with a full quota of wars and heroic
action (as in the life of Samson); stories of adventure and
intrigue in vivid oriental surroundings (as in the Book of
Esther) conflict, love and revenge—none of which finds
much place in the New Testament. The Hebrew Scriptures
are religious without being ecclesiastical. They deal with the
ways of God to Man in this world and say little or nothing
about the life of the world to come. Here is where it may
come to terms with the secular drama which likewise leaves
out the life of the world to come as essentially without

dramatic interest. J. C. Powys has remarked on "the human wisdom, the human sensuality, the human anger, the human justice, the human magnanimity, the human triumph, of this old shameless literature of the Old Testament." The old English dramatists were aware of this, and it attracted them to this book in preference to the New Testament. The old play of *Jacob and Esau* is a good example of this, and an even better instance is George Peele's *The Love of King David and Fair Bethsabe* (1599). This is not a Miracle Play or a Morality but a piece of " straight " Elizabethan theatre written in the new popular blank-verse and celebrating all the barbaric, exciting, and romantic history of the House of David—the incestuous love of Amnon for Tamar: the revolt of Absalom: the adultery of David with Bathsheba: the violent dramatic spectacle of Absalom hanging by his hair: the pathetic sorrows of David: the just retribution that overtakes him. The drums and trumpets of the captains of the hosts, the music of the banquet, and the dance and song of the shepherds, are the vivid accompaniment of a story of crime and punishment, which, whilst being essentially a moral story, a story of the ways of God to sinful man, is nevertheless also a human tragedy, a piece of ready-made dramatic material which might have attracted for its handling a greater dramatist than Peele.

This however takes us beyond the strictly medieval field. In the Morality plays which succeeded the Miracles and Mysteries of the earlier Middle Ages, there are no obvious Jews, but there is nevertheless the influence of both types of Jew-character, the Devil-Jew and the Jew-Hero. In the fifteenth century Morality Play of *Everyman* we find a story of sinfulness, retribution, and repentance essentially of the Old Testament pattern and highly reminiscent of the career of David as dramatised by Peele. At the end of his life, Strength promises Everyman to

> be as sure by thee
> As ever I was by Judas Maccabee.

And there is an even stronger link between this play and Jewish tradition, for the late Rev. S. Singer surmised that the source of the story is ultimately to be traced to the allegory of Everyman in the thirty-fourth chapter of the early rabbinic work, *Pirke de Rabbi Eleazar*, which reads very like the basic plot of this English dramatic piece.

The good Jew thus lurks in the background of the Morality plays determining its inspiration to some extent —but the bad Jew is more obviously in the foreground in the figure of the Devil and his Vice, the villain and clown respectively of the Morality tradition. The latter are generally represented as Jews in their costume and their habits of speech. In the play of *St. Mary Magdalen*, the Vice announces his name as " moysaical Justice." The Devil's resemblance to, if not identity with, the Jew has already been noted. Together they serve to perpetuate in the popular imagination that Judas-Judaeus-Satan combination which is to be eventually bequeathed to the secular drama of Marlowe and Shakespeare, to the nineteenth century novelists, and to the writings of Graham Greene and T. S. Eliot nearer our own days. Judas, Shylock, Fagin, and Colleoni represent a persistent tradition, a coherent and elaborate myth which, for detailed continuity, has few parallels in literary history. The Devil and the Vice of the old Morality Play provide the essential link between the modern and medieval manifestations of that myth.

The Poets

The non-dramatic literature of the Medieval Ages is hardly less rich in Jewish "types" than the Miracles. Mysteries, and Moralities. Chaucer's *Prioress's Tale* is a curious mixture of realism and mythology. The poem, though composed about one hundred years after the expulsion of Jews from England, is not without a realistic background acquired perhaps through Chaucer's travels abroad in France and Italy. He begins with a typical "Jewerye" of

Jews' Street of the day in some " greet citee." It was, he
says,

> Sustened by a lord of that countree
> For foule usure and lucre of villenye
> Hateful to Christ and to his compaignye.
> And thurgh the strete men myghte ride or wende.
> For it was free and open at eyther ende.

It is a story of how a Christian boy who made a practice of
walking through the Jewry singing the hymn " Alma
Redemptoris Mater " eventually enraged the Jewish in-
habitants to such an extent that they conceived the diabolical plan of murdering him. When they had carried out
their plan, they cast him into a pit. His mother, a widow,
goes out to look for him and eventually arrives at the pit:
there a miracle takes place, and the dead child is enabled
to reveal his whereabouts by bursting out once again into
pious hymn-singing—this in spite of his throat being cut.
A crowd gathers, and the Provost deals summarily with
the case. The Jews are bound and punished " with torment
and with shameful deeth echon." The background of the
tale is the ritual-murder libel which began in England in
the twelfth century, with the story that the Jews had *crucified* a boy called William in Norwich. A later example
from the thirteenth century is referred to by Chaucer towards the end of his tale where he mentions,

> yonge Hugh of Lyncoln, slayn also
> With cursed Jewes, as it is notable.

The medieval mind found no difficulty in accepting this
ritual-murder story as part of the Jewish myth: it was an
age essentially aprioristic in its attitude to history. If the
Jews had crucified Jesus, it was natural that they should
go on doing so either by killing young children at the
Passover season or by wickedly pricking the sacramental
wafer and causing the body of the crucified Lord to bleed
afresh. Empirical verification was not particularly necessary in this case, any more than it was necessary to prove
by reference to the facts that heavy objects fell to the

ground more quickly than light ones—such facts followed deductively from the nature of things. There would be a certain naïf charm about such fantasies, if they were not occasionally somewhat macabre—as in the present example. It must be said, however, that the shading in this particular tale is not all dark—some of the lighter side of Chaucer's medieval fancy is also in evidence, as in the pretty picture of the seven-year-old infant, the wonder of the auditors when the miracle is performed, and the prayer to the martyred saints at the end. Also the reader is expected to appreciate it as the tale of the naïvely pious Prioress with her finickiness and superstitious credulity.

The ballads of this period were even closer to popular tradition than Chaucer's *Canterbury Tales* and they give us the current concept of the Jew with greater baldness and less fancy and sentiment than Chaucer's Prioress displays. In Percy's collection of early poetry, there is an old Scottish ballad probably of the fourteenth century, entitled, *The Jew's Daughter*. This too is evidently inspired by the alleged ritual murder of Hugh of Lincoln. Again we have the Christian schoolboy who has wandered into the Jewry. The murder this time is committed by a young Jewess armed with a pen-knife and " an apple reid and white " to " intice the yong thing in." We may well wonder why the ritual-murder libel, so frequently repudiated by the Popes themselves, continued to attract the medieval poet, or indeed why, when so many medieval legends have died a natural death in the course of the centuries, this particular one should have survived into modern times as a stimulus to mob violence against the Jews in Damascus, in Kiev, or in Berlin? It is clearly a very necessary and intimate part of the myth, this charge of blood-guilt which persists in the face of every effort to disprove or dispel it. From a logical point of view the charge is made more paradoxical by the fact that whilst, unfortunately, hundreds of thousands of cases are known of Jews being murdered by gentiles for their Jewish faith, there is virtually no example on record of a *gentile* having been murdered by a Jew on account of his *Christian* faith. This paradox, whilst deepening the mystery from a logical point of view, solves it from a psychological point of view. One does not require to be an expert psychologist to recognise in this a simple example of guilt transference or substitution. The guilt one feels in one's own conscience (in this case blood guilt) is transferred imaginatively to the victim who is made guilty of precisely the same crime. In this way the burden of guilt is diverted, whilst at the same time the crime is obscurely justified by being visualised as a punishment for a previous crime committed by the victim! The mass-murder of the Jews recorded towards the end of the *Prioress's Tale* is, in a psychological sense, not the end of the tale but its beginning. It is no accident that the revival of the blood-libel has always been associated with actual outbreaks of violence against the Jews: the myth is clearly produced to justify by anticipation the crime already meditated in the unconscious. "Murdered as they so often were," says Sinsheimer, "there must be blood-guilt upon them—such was medieval logic." Medieval logic is, however, unfortunately not confined to the Middle Ages.

A similar example of a psychological tangle involving transference is to be found in the medieval legend of *The Wandering Jew*. This popular story has survived into modern times. In the English romantic period we find (favourable) treatments of the theme in Shelley and Wordsworth. An early medieval version was known to Matthew Paris in the thirteenth century: but the better known version is to be found in Percy's collection evidently based on a sixteenth century German model. Jesus is pictured on his way to Calvary carrying his cross. Exhausted by his labours he seeks to rest on a stone occupied by an unsympathetic Jew:

> Being weary thus, he sought for rest
> To ease his burdened soule,
> Upon a stone ; the which a wretch
> Did churlishly controule . . .
> And thereupon he thrust him thence ;

> At which our Saviour sayd,
> ' I sure will rest, but thou shalt walke,
> And have no journey stayd.'
> With that this cursed shoemaker,
> For offering Christ this wrong
> Left wife and children, house and all,
> And went from thence along ...
> So doth this wandring Jew,
> From place to place, but cannot rest
> For seeing countries newe.

And so the Jewish shoemaker wanders on through the centuries, a little like the *Ancient Mariner* of Coleridge's poem (which may have been collaterally inspired by the Wandering Jew legend), and carrying on his back the curse of the dying God, the curse of immortality! Here we may suspect the medieval imagination is trying to come to terms with the phenomenon of the persistence of the Jew in spite of persecution and exile. By a simple transference, the power of survival possessed by the Jew is seen not as a testimony to his own fortitude and spiritual integrity, but as a testimony to Christian truth. It should be remarked at this point that the tone of the ballad is not entirely hostile—the Wandering Jew is in his way an impressive figure. Something of the Wandering Jew adheres to Bloom in James Joyce's *Ulysses*. His immortality may be a curse but it confers upon him a certain dignity, which the poet having as it were explained away to his own satisfaction, is now free to acknowledge. In recognising him, the Christian medieval imagination pays its respects to the patriarchal Jew, the symbol of mankind's historical continuity—for the Jew comes into the medieval world carrying upon himself the burden of a hoary antiquity reaching back to the creation of the world, and the burden of a futurity reaching forward by promise to the end of days. Read in this sense, the words,

I sure will rest, but thou shalt walke

carry with them a suggestion of repining and regret and not a little sense of humility before the mystery of the eternal Jew.

CHAPTER TWO

THE TUDOR PERIOD AND BEYOND

Marlowe and Shakespeare

We have already remarked on the fact that, with the secularization of the Drama, the crucifixion story and the Jew's part or supposed part in it, lose in dramatic interest. There are no Passion plays written in the Age of Shakespeare. The subject was thought to be too sacred. But there is a fresh comprehension and appreciation of the literature of the Old Testament owing to the Reformation discovery of Scripture and its wide diffusion in the vernacular. We would expect then that a more sympathetic representation of the Jew on the stage would take the place of the old Judas-Devil image. Indeed, some sympathetic representations do occur. In R. Wilson's *Three Ladies of London* (first printed 1584) there is a trial scene between the Jew Gerontus and a Christian merchant before " the Judge of Turkie." In this scene it is Mercadore the Christian who shows up worst by defrauding the Jew of his money which he has wasted on luxuries. The Jew for his part refuses to press the rigour of the law against the Christian out of respect for the latter's religious profession, and lets his claim go as a bad debt. It is noteworthy that in this example the broken English is given to the Christian Mercadore (who is in literal fact a Merchant of Venice), whilst Gerontus speaks the most polite English of the play:

> Stay there most puissant Judge. Senior Mercadorus,
> consider what you doo,
> Pay me the principall, as for the interest I forgive it you:

And yet the interest is allowed amongst you Christians, as
well as in Turky,
Therefore respect your faith, and do not seeme to deceive me.

Mercadore replies: " No point da interest, no point da
principall." In Shakespeare's play the moral balance
between the two parties, the Jew and the Christian, is
reversed (although in a legal sense Shylock might have
as good a claim as Gerontus). There are possible echoes in
Shakespeare's play of the above-quoted passage which
suggest that Shakespeare knew this rather wooden allegorical play and had been impressed by the trial scene even
whilst he may have felt that the Jew was being treated
with unnatural delicacy. One of the points in this speech
which we should notice and which is important for a proper
understanding of *The Merchant of Venice* is the phrase
" And yet the interest is allowed amongst you Christians."
The Three Ladies of London is very much a polemic
against usury, and Wilson is going out of his way to
indicate that this is not exclusively, or even primarily, a
Jewish vice. It is in fact part of the new economic order
of the sixteenth century, necessitated by the expansion of
commerce and exploration, and legitimated in the Calvinist scheme of civil society. If, in Shakespeare's play,
the responsibility for this evil (as it was thought) is laid
at the door of the Jew—the fury and bitterness of the
attack upon usance, as expressed by Antonio and others,
is to be explained by the reaction against current social
and economic developments by no means originating in
Jewry. This is another example of guilt transference.

But before we turn to a detailed examination of Shakespeare's play we must consider one remarkable and monstrous portrayal of the Jew by a dramatist of genius, namely
Shakespeare's most brilliant contemporary, Christopher
Marlowe, in his *The Jew of Malta* (1589?). From this
play, it is obvious that the medieval Judas-Devil picture
is still very much alive. Marlowe whilst being an enlightened Renaissance man, a revolutionary, a personality
of the new era, nevertheless had his ear very close to the

ground and could catch the vibrations of folk tradition. Thus *Doctor Faustus* (1588?) owes much to the Morality Play tradition and contains a very medieval pageant of the Seven Deadly Sins. And in *The Jew of Malta* the characterisation of Barabas owes much to this old-fashioned appeal of the melodramatic villain with red hair and beard, artificial nose and appropriate costume. The old ritual-murder theme is recalled in the question of Friar Jacomo (Act III), " What, has he crucified a child? " It addition, his account of his way of life given to his newly-found servant, Ithamore, in Act II, establishes Barabas securely in the old tradition of medieval anti-semitic fantasy :

> As for myself I walk abroad o'nights
> And kill sick people groaning under walls :
> Sometimes I go about and poison wells ;
> And now and then, to cherish Christian thieves,
> I am content to lose some of my crowns,
> That I may, walking in my gallery,
> See 'em go pinion'd along by my door.
> Being young, I studied physic, and began
> To practise first upon the Italian ;
> There I enrich'd the priests with burials,
> And always kept the sexton's arms in ure,
> With digging graves and ringing dead men's knells :
> And after that, was I an engineer,
> And in the wars 'twixt France and Germany,
> Under pretence of helping Charles the Fifth,
> Slew friend and enemy with my stratagems :
> Then after that was I an usurer,
> And with extorting, cozening, forfeiting,
> And tricks belonging unto brokery,
> I fill'd the gaols with bankrupts in a year,
> And with young orphans planted hospitals, . . .

The poisoning of the wells was an old medieval charge against the Jews—a prelogical explanation of the origin of the Plague. The serious intent has gone with Marlowe —who could not have believed this story any longer— and the whole passage is little more than an exercise in sensational rhetoric, a display of melodramatic horrors which the Elizabethans enjoyed in much the same way as modern cinema audiences enjoy certain incredible films of the horrific kind. Marlowe dealt consciously in hyperbole as a means of liberating poetic energy, and his audience enjoyed the poetry and the thrills without ever seriously expecting to encounter a Jew remotely resembling Barabas, with his medieval bellyful of horrors.

All this would be merely to stress the traditional character of the portrait of Barabas, its appeal to the folk tradition of anti-semitism. But if that were all that Barabas had to offer us there would be little to explain the attraction of the theme for Marlowe, the young iconoclast and free-thinker, with his revolutionary Renaissance ardour and his interest in all the new currents which were stirring in the age of the first Elizabeth. Such a man was the author of *Tamburlaine* and *Doctor Faustus,* and a spirit no less fiery and adventurous is to be discerned in *The Jew of Malta.* In the passage just quoted, the reference to Barabas's career as a physician is, we may suppose, part of his traditional medieval character: the reference to his exploits as an " engineer " is more surprising, especially as he goes on to explain that he had made use of his skill to manage great political schemes in the wars between France and Germany! Into the portrait of Barabas goes Mar-lowe's fascination for the new political philosophy of Machiavellianism, with its novelty, and moral (or we might say, immoral) radicalism. *The Jew of Malta* is in fact explicitly concerned with portraying the influence of the diabolical Machiavelli: and the plays opens with a prologue pronouned by the ghost of Machiavelli himself who begs the audience to give Barabas a fair hearing " because he favours me." Again, Marlowe is not overtly recommending Machiavelli, but the portrait has for him as positive a value as the portrait of Mephistopheles in *Doctor Faustus*, which undoubtedly carries with it likewise an intimate part of Marlowe's own personality.

All this, we might think, takes us very far from contemporary Jews, or indeed Jews of any period. Machiavellianism was after all a fruit of the Renaissance in Italy: it may be traced back also to Polybius and the ancient Pagan humanists. If anything, it may be regarded as a revolt *against* the Jewish ethic rather than an exemplification of it. How then does Marlowe come to take the Jew Barabas as his model for a " Machiavellian politician "? We shall understand the identification better when we realise that for Marlowe Machiavellianism was not so much a science of politics as a new and daring employment of *power,* and the appeal of it for him was what the appeal of atomic power would be to a man of imagination today. Barabas demonstrates how the new politician through the exercise of the new wealth and through the exercise of a grand strategy, involving the movements of men and armies, may bring about great and mighty changes in the world. We see Barabas arranging for the conquest of Malta by the Turks, and then turning against the Turks only to be hoist in the end by his own petard when the Christians learn to employ his own policy against him. All this was thrilling and new. It meant an end of the old dynastic control of international affairs and the irruption of the individual, the middle-class merchant, into the sphere of government. Marlowe felt (as a middle-class adventurer himself who had dabbled just a little in international conspiracy) that somehow the future belonged not to kings and courts but to powerful politicians possessing energy and imagination. If we detach the elements of incredible evil from Barabas (those elements which come from his medieval background) we see him as an essentially modern figure, a symbol of the new industrial and political power which was to emerge in the course of the next two centuries in Western Europe and America.

Again we may ask, what had the Jew to do with *this* development? And the answer is that for Marlowe and his contemporaries one famous Jew had indeed become a symbol of such power. He was Joseph Nasi, Duke of Naxos—a Marrano refugee from Portugal who played a leading *rôle* as the most influential adviser of the Sultan of Turkey in his struggle against the Christian West in the sixteenth century. The most sensational success he had was in engineering the capture of Cyprus by the Turks in 1570 (when it next changed hands in the nineteenth century, another Jewish politician, Disraeli, was principally involved). Joseph Nasi was a figure of very great note throughout Europe: it was known that he had a tremendous intelligence service recruited from amongst his Marrano friends who shared his hatred of Spain and the Catholic powers. Nasi's services to Turkey were not remembered when a new Sultan acceded in 1574—as in the case of his great Biblical namesake, the new pharaoh knew not Joseph—and he was suffered to die without the honours he deserved. The Englishman's feelings about this great struggle going on in the Mediterranean were certainly mixed, but we cannot believe that Marlowe and his contemporaries were without sympathy for Joseph, the declared enemy of England's principal rival, Spain. Certainly Barabas is a monstrous portrait, a caricature: he bears no resemblance to the historical Joseph Nasi, except in the sense that they were both figures of power, but we may suspect that in some perverted way, disguised even from himself, Marlowe is in this play paying his respects to the Jew of the new age who has burst the shackles of medieval Christendom and found a field large enough for the exercise of his energies and the realisation of his vision.

Two particular features of the portrayal of the Jew in this play deserve incidental notice before we pass on to the Jew play of Marlowe's more illustrious colleague, Shakespeare, for we shall see that both these features are reproduced in Shakespeare's play. In the first place, Barabas has a daughter, Abigail, not indeed altogether exempt from her father's political villainies, but " matchless beautiful "

> As, had you seen her 'twould have mov'd your heart,

Though countermin'd with walls of brass, to love,
Or at least, to pity.

These words are spoken by her lover Mathias, a Christian to whom she remains faithful in thought (though not in word) throughout the play. She seeks to retire to a nunnery after the death of Mathias, only to be pursued by her father's machinations and secretly poisoned.

This division of the Jew's domestic set-up into the black father, and the white, pure, and beautiful daughter is repeated in Shakespeare's play in the characters of Shylock and Jessica where we see once again this polarisation, as it were, of the Jewish soul in Father and Daughter. It is true that in both cases the beautiful daughter of the Jew is seen to embrace Christianity and abandon her faithless progenitor, but whence the need to portray the Jew as having a daughter capable of better things? Is there not perhaps here at work something of the dual image? There are no good characters in the family of Lucifer, no good angel issues from the Devil—but the Jew is shown as capable of giving birth to youth and beauty, as capable of being redeemed through his offspring. The same pattern is repeated later on, as we shall see, in Scott's *Ivanhoe* in the characters of Isaac and Rebecca. Perhaps this represents a secularised and sentimentalised version of that Christian paradox about the Jew first formulated by Paul in the parable of the olive tree whose branches will one day be restored to the uncorrupted native root.

The second interesting feature is the grouping of the Jew and his servant. In Marlowe it is the slave Ithamore; in Shakespeare, we find Shylock set off by the clown, Launcelot Gobbo. In both cases one important function of the Jew's servant is obvious—it is to direct the audience's laughter against the Jew, to point out the joke every time the Jew appears (" O brave! master, I worship your nose for this "), though Launcelot is a more polished and successful clown than Ithamore who really deals in crude farce. This relation between the Jew and his servant which

seems to be necessary to uphold the Jew's *rôle* as a comic
figure is evidently an inheritance from the Morality play
where the Devil is accompanied by his Vice or clown.
Michelson remarks, " The Devil is generally accompanied
by the Vice, . . . when Devil and Vice appear no longer
on stage in the regular drama, their places are taken by
the Jew and his servant. The Vice belabours his master
the Devil, the Jew is always poked fun at, or taken in by
his servant ". And he concludes further on that *The Merchant of Venice,* with Shylock and Launcelot functioning
still in some sort as the Devil and Vice of the play, is a
kind of late Morality play. We may surmise that the function of the Vice is to prevent the Devil from becoming a
tragic hero (this happened more or less in Milton's *Paradise
Lost* where it is notable that Milton failed to introduce a
comic character into Satan's *entourage*), and the same
is probably true of the Jew and his Servant. The comic
character (and note that he is a *non-Jew*) exists to prevent
the isolation and pride of the Jew from becoming the focus
of tragic pathos.

But if this is the intention in Shakespeare's *Merchant
of Venice,* then it is obvious to every reader and spectator
that the trick does not succeed. Or, to put it more correctly,
the attempt is abandoned half-way; Launcelot passes out
of the Jew's domestic circle, and Shylock is left alone and
permitted to rise to tragic dignity in the latter half of
the play.

A true understanding of Shakespeare's play allows us
to see Shylock both as the heir of the monstrous, bloodthirsty, usurer-murderer of medieval legend filtered through
stage melodrama, and also as Shakespeare's serious study
of the Jewish problem imaged in a figure of tragic dimen-
sions, hated and hating, but above all things, human.
Through Shylock, the evil portrait of the Jew, the Judas-
myth, the ritual murder legend (for make no mistake,
Shylock desires to kill Antonio, and desires to kill him
because he is a Christian — " I hate him for he is a
Christian ") are perpetuated into the modern world: but

also in Shylock the Jew is seen—and not the Biblical Jew but the Jew of current history—for the first time in modern literature as a human being. He has been to that extent, demythologised:

> I am a Jew. Hath not a Jew eyes? hath not a Jew hands, organs, dimensions, senses, affections, passions? fed with the same food, hurt with the same weapons, subject to the same diseases, healed by the same means, warmed and cooled by the same winter and summer, as a Christian is? If you prick us, do we not bleed? if you tickle us, do we not laugh? if you poison us, do we not die? and if you wrong us, shall we not revenge?

This is the extent of Shakespeare's achievement. One could go further and say with Dover Wilson that through grappling seriously with the Jew, Shylock, Shakespeare found himself in the fullest sense as a student of human character in its tragic phase. *The Merchant of Venice* leads forward to *Hamlet* and *Antony and Cleopatra*. There are two Shylocks of stage history: one popularised by Irving shows him as " a great tragic figure, representative of the suffering Hebrew race throughout history and expressing the indignation and the aspirations of oppressed peoples and races throughout the world." The older tradition current at the time of Shakespeare is that " of a comic character, of a devil in the likeness of an old Jew, a crafty bloodthirsty villain, crying out for revenge upon a decent Christian gentleman." And Professor Wilson concludes that "Shakespeare intended both Shylocks. He inherited a Jew play upon which he constructed *The Merchant*, and he developed the character he found therein. He loaded the dice still more heavily against him; he made him more bloodthirsty than before . . . Yet the other Shylock was also Shakespeare's from the start, the conscious product of his genius, deliberately set forth for the judicious to ponder." To what extent Shakespeare *consciously* intended to portray Shylock at two levels, would be difficult to determine. Something similar happens in other plays, in the portrayal of Angelo in *Measure for Measure,* or even in *Hamlet,* where an old revenge-melodrama with an incredible villain and a rather clownish hero is caught up and transformed into a psychological tragedy of perennial fascination and a tragedy of incomparable depth and subtlety; and yet at the same time, the structure and machinery of old melodrama remain, the Ghost roaring for revenge, the graveyard scene, the fine thrill and horror of the ending. In *The Merchant of Venice* we find a similar co-existence of old popular elements, and new deeper interest. Shakespeare is neither prophet nor moralist: he was content to use the old stage-Jew as colourful dramatic material, but neither his literary genius, nor his sense of human truth and credibility permitted him to rest totally satisfied with it. The result is this disturbing and moving play, in which the Jew is laughed on at the beginning and hooted off at the end; but in the course of his passage across the stage, he questions the principles and convictions upon which the gentile society around him is based.

It is often said that in Shylock, Shakespeare penetrated into the psychology of the Jew. There *is* something Jewish about him certainly, or shall we say something of the Jew of the *Galut,* in his dark and gloomy resentments, his feverish care for his possessions, his sense of family (he prizes the jewel left him by his dead wife), his loyalty to his fellow Jews, his love of his daughter, his gestures, his faith in the absolute validity of the written bond (the stress on this is a master-stroke), his appeal to law as against sentiment. But when all this has been said, it is still questionable whether Shylock is really a Jew, and this not so much because of the un-Jewish characteristics Shakespeare bestows upon him (especially his bloodthirstiness) as because of what is omitted, namely the whole region of Jewish spirituality. He is a Jew without Judaism. Shylock's appeal to Scripture, in the story of Laban's flocks, or in his reference to Portia as " A Daniel come to judgment," are not sufficient to conceal the total lack of religious depth in the character of Shylock. He is to that extent a Jew seen from the outside: there is no hint in him of the

Jew's faith, of his blind and mystical devotion to the *Torah*; there is nothing of his covenant-bonds, of his sense of a religious destiny beside which all his worldly goods are merely vanity. To expect Shakespeare to produce such a portrait in the absence of any real knowledge of Jews and of Jewish life would be to expect the impossible. As far as the portrait of the Jew is concerned, Shakespeare does everything that is possible to humanise and explicate him, whilst leaving out the tap-root of his historical existence. It is as though he had made the very best possible job of *Hamlet* whilst omitting the Prince. How then was it possible to affirm as we have done, that *The Merchant of Venice* is a serious study of the Jewish problem?

The answer is that Shakespeare's dramatic genius leads him to construct a perfect pattern of *relationships between his characters,* even when not doing full justice to the history and motives of the characters themselves. Thus *The Merchant* gives us a classical, and, I think, well-nigh perfect illustration of the position of the Jew in the gentile environment, of the tensions and difficulties produced by his position, and of his vain attempts to employ gentile law and custom in order to break out of the vicious circle set up by the gentile need of him on the one hand, and contempt for his person on the other. Shakespeare penetrates to the Christian hatred of the Jew as the source of Shylock's plot against Antonio : he shows him for a moment seriously trying to win Antonio's love and respect, but being spurned. The crisis comes when he is bereaved of his daughter through the treachery of one of Antonio's Christian friends. The movement mounting up to the trial scene at the climax of the play proceeds as a sort of relentless closing in upon Shylock who reacts rather like a hunted animal with the hunters closing in upon it, or a bear being baited to the point of fury. Such is the main pattern. But in the trial scene the Jew is not merely a hunted animal who is borne down and overthrown by his adversaries after trying to inflict injury upon them; he throws out a moral challenge to the Christian world. To the Duke's demand that he show mercy and surrender his bond, Shylock forcefully rejoins:

> You have among you many a purchased slave,
> Which, like your asses and your dogs and mules,
> You use in abject and in slavish parts,
> Because you bought them: shall I say to you,
> Let them be free, marry them to your heirs?

This demand for tempering justice with mercy is shown to be extremely relevant to Christian society, and Shylock's implied criticism of slavery in the above-cited passage— the high-water mark of Shakeapeare's social ethic—is unanswerable It has even been suggested that Portia's great speech, addressed to Shylock:

> The quality of mercy is not strained

is subtly intended as an appeal not so much to Shylock as to Shakespeare's compatriots, the Queen and her counsellors, whose judicial proceedings were very often not above reproach. There had been for instance the very questionable judicial proceedings against Mary Queen of Scots in 1587. The reference in the speech to mercy as the proper attribute of monarchs (" it becomes/The throned monarch better than his crown ") shows that kings and queens are very much in his mind. It has even been suggested that Shakespeare is glancing at a contemporary perversion of justice in the trial and execution of a Marrano Jew, Roderigo Lopez in 1594, at the instigation of the Earl of Essex. The charge (unsubstantiated by genuine evidence) was of high treason and the attempted murder of the Queen. The Queen herself (who seems later to have regretted her part in the proceedings) may have been gently alluded to in Portia's remark:

> And earthly power doth then show likest God's
> When mercy seasons justice.

Certainly no-one would suggest that Shakespeare was on the side of Lopez and against Essex and his faction, but we may see in this play something of an attempt to penetrate to the human issues involved and temper some of the darker prejudices aroused at the time with an infusion of reason and sensibility. If in the course of this, the Jew rather than his persecutors becomes the man of blood to whom the sermon on tolerance must be preached, we have here again an example of that guilt-transference which is common to the portrayal of the Jew in Shakespeare, Marlowe, and Chaucer.

Shylock goes off at the end of Act IV defeated and dishonoured but there is no doubt that he has won for himself, if only because of the injuries he has suffered, something of the audience's sympathy. Much the same thing happens to Malvolio at the end of *Twelfth Night,* and it is notable that the two characters have something in common. Both are representatives of the Middle Class vainly struggling to establish themselves in an environment still dominated by chivalric modes and aristocratic privilege. Both have a certain Puritan kill-joy attitude (see *The Merchant,* Act II, scene v) and Shylock's profession of usurer is as typical of the new Calvinist economics as of medieval Jewry. It might be argued that Shylock is a man of the new world, vital, energetic, realistic, and seeing through all the surface pretences of the more charming order of society based on birth and station. Throughout the play the cash nexus is shown as controlling even the lives of the upper class. Romance and money cannot be separated. " In Belmont is a lady richly left." This plays a part in Bassanio's calculations. He goes in search of the golden fleece: but he needs money for the expedition, and so he borrows from the Jew. Romantic love becomes a business venture which pays dividends if you are lucky. Jessica running off with her lover does not forget to take the ducats with her. Shakespeare is using the Jew for the purpose of giving to the moonlit world of medieval enchantment a more prosaic aspect. The ambiguity in the characterisation of Shylock is thus manifold. As a Judas figure he is a medieval relic—an echo no longer credible of the old Mystery plays and Moralities; but as the alien Jew demanding equal rights, fiercely impeaching his enemies in the name of their common humanity, and seeking power through the new economic forces, he is essentially a symbol of the future, of a world in which Antonio, Lorenzo, and the romantic idyll of Portia and her lovers at Belmont, will have little or no place.

Poets and Prose Writers

Outside the field of Drama, the Jew occupies an incidental rôle in Elizabethan literature. The first English novel (as it is sometimes described), Thomas Nashe's *The Unfortunate Traveller* (1594), a picaresque tale of adventure set in the early sixteenth century, contains two Jewish characters of the blackest hue, Zadoch and Zachary. Zachary is a physician who buys a couple of live Christians (in fact the hero Jack Wilton and his sweetheart Diamante) from Zadoch for the purpose of anatomical dissection! We seem to be back here with the ritual murder legend, but now farcically exaggerated and stripped of its supposed religious character. The Jews are eventually exposed, and Zadoch suffers hanging and torture, an episode described in abundant and gruesome detail. The outstanding features here, the Jewish practice of medicine, the charge of poisoning, the execution of one of the malefactors at the end, would be enough to link the story firmly with the Lopez sensation of the same year. Nashe was indeed the ancestor of the crime journalist of our modern Sunday papers, but here enabled to give his imagination free rein by transposing the Jew Lopez to the realm of pure fantasy. The evil portrayal of the Jew in this fiction is to prove ominous for the English novel of the future. The good Jew (as in Scott and George Eliot) is going to be the exception down to the end of the nineteenth century.

In other forms of prose, in Robert Greene's moral tales for instance, the case is different. He has at least two such tracts relevant to our inquiry; one of them, *The Myrrour of Modestie* (1584), tells the apocryphal story of Susannah and the Elders, making much of the wickedness of the two lecherous judges, but also much of the purity and piety of this daughter of Israel whose whole delight was in the Law of God. The tale is written in the now fashionable artificial euphuistic prose, first popularised by Lyly, but it has a vivid and racy narrative movement, and testifies to the abiding interest of the Old Testament literature as imaginative source material. A few years later, he produced a penitential tract (as a lament for his own sinful youth), entitled, *Greene's Mourning Garment*; this is based on the New Testament parable of the prodigal son with an obvious application to all spendthrifts and as a dissuasive against travel and women. From our point of view, the most interesting character is the hero's father Rabbi Bilessi, whose wise axioms (not ultimately followed) are bestowed on the young man before he sets out on his travels. Bilessi's wisdom is fabulous:

> Honour had pitcht her pauilion in his tresses, and the tramells of his hair were full of reuerence: his countenance graue, as became his yeares, and yet full of lenity; that as the Eagle hath talents [sc. talons] to strike, and wings to shadow: so his lookes carried threats to chastise, and favours to incourage. This old man being thus grac'd by Nature and fortune, hath the gifts of the minde so interlarded with the excellence of all vertues, that if *Aristotle* had been aliue, he would haue confest this *Rabbi* to haue attained to the perfection of the *summum bonum*.

The portrait looks forward to Disraeli's picture of Sidonia, the Jewish superman who similarly was the exemplar of all the virtues, especially the philosophical ones. We need not take Greene's repentance too seriously, and this tract turns out to be rather dull and repetitive. Rabbi Bilessi does not really come to life, nor are we led to believe that as a Jewish symbol he meant very much either to Greene or to his audience.

It is in the religious poetry of the seventeenth century that the Christian imagination first seriously evaluates the

Jew as a positive figure, or at least first seriously tries to resolve the contradiction between the negative and positive aspects of the traditional portrait. It is pleasant to record that the first genuinely and deeply sympathetic poem on the Jew comes from the pen of the gentlest of English priests and the most simple, delicate, and masculine of English seventeenth century poets. George Herbert's collection of lyrics. *The Temple* (published 1633) contains many paraphrases of the *Psalms* and as religious poetry owes more than a little to the Hebrew Biblical tradition of meditation. His poem, *The Jews,* therefore, comes as an explicit acknowledgment of the sources of his own poetic, and devotional inspiration:

> Poor nation, whose sweet sap and juice
> Our scions have purloin'd, and left you dry:
> Whose streams we got by the Apostles' sluice,
> And use in baptism, while ye pine and die:
> Who by not keeping once, became a debtor;
> And now by keeping lose the letter.
>
> O that my prayers! mine, alas!
> O that some Angel might a trumpet sound:
> At which the Church falling upon her face
> Should cry so loud, until the trump were drown'd,
> And by that cry of her dear Lord obtain,
> That your sweet sap might come again!

The reference to "sap," "juice," and "scions" indicates the origin of the poem's imagery in Paul's parable of the good olive tree which shall one day have its own branches (*i.e.,* the remnant of Israel) restored to it. This is a Christian poem, the theme of which is the conversion of the Jew to Christianity when " the fulness of the Gentiles be come in," but it is nevertheless a poem which breathes a devout love of Israel as the people of God.

Henry Vaughan's poem of the same title was modelled upon Herbert's, but breathes a more passionate strain. It likewise deserves lengthy quotation:

When the fair year
Of your deliverer comes,
And that long frost which now benumbs
Your hearts shall thaw ; when Angels here
Shall yet to man appear,
And familiarly confer
Beneath the Oke and Juniper :
When the bright *Dove*
Which now these many, many Springs
Hath kept above,
Shall with spread wings
Descend, and living waters flow
To make drie dust, and dead trees grow ;

O then that I
Might live, and see the Olive bear
Her proper branches ! which now lie
Scattered each where,
And without root and sap decay
Cast by the husband-man away.
And sure it is not far !
For as your fast and foul decays
Forerunning the bright morning-star,
Did sadly note his healing rayes
Would shine elsewhere, since you were blind,
And would be cross, when God was kinde :
So by all signs
Our fulness too is now come in,
And the same Sun which here declines
And sets, will few hours hence begin
To rise on you again, and look
Towards old *Mamre* and *Eshcols* brook.

The reproach to Israel is no longer uttered in the form
of a curse but as a sad regret at missed opportunities
(" since you were blind / And would be cross, when God
was kinde "). Herbert and Vaughan devoted their literary
genius to the service of a movement in English life and
literature which is sometimes termed the Anglican *via
media*. This owed much to the Reformation rediscovery
of Scripture and the evangelical revival of the sixteenth
century, but its spirit was tolerant and undogmatic.
Herbert himself in his prose work, *A Priest to the Temple*,

stressed the need for practical divinity, and this tendency is evident too among such contemporaries as Bishops Joseph Hall and Jeremy Taylor. And as one might expect, this practical emphasis on the carrying out of the commandments and on the performance of acts of piety led to a more sympathetic appreciation of the Hebrew religious temper than had been possible with Luther and the early reformers. Joseph Hall preached a sermon on the Pharisees in which, perhaps for the first time, they are treated with some respect, and Jeremy Taylor appeals to the law of the Old Testament as the basis of morality. It is no coincidence that the religious humanists of the mid-seventeenth century such as Jeremy Taylor and (from the Puritan side) Milton, should have helped to create a social and religious climate, in which the admission of the Jews and the subsequent normalisation of their status should have become possible. They themselves were not concerned in the movement for re-admitting the Jews, but the new non-evangelical currents in religious life which they manifest, owing their inspiration very much to the Old Testament (which Milton was able to read in the Hebrew), combined with a humanist respect for liberty and freedom of conscience, to give an impetus to all such liberal tendencies. A Puritan such as Roger Williams was at this time arguing for toleration of Jews as a Christian principle.

The greatest humanist as well as the greatest Hebraist among seventeenth century writers was the poet Milton, and it is therefore not surprising that he should have written the two most famous English poems on Old Testament subjects namely, *Paradise Lost* and *Samson Agonistes*. The former of these is not strictly relevant to the subject of the portrayal of the Jew in English literature; the latter may be mentioned as continuing the tradition of secular drama based on the lives of the Old Testament heroes. We noticed examples in the Middle Ages and we remarked on Peele's *David and Bethsabe*. In Milton's *Samson* we have the noblest work in this *genre* in the English language.

Milton's own Hebraic temper and his sense of personal dedication as a kind of prophet or herald appointed to assist the regeneration of the English nation, led him to identify himself with the great heroes and prophets of Jewish antiquity. This identification is most apparent in his drama of Samson where his picture of the captive Israelite leader—

Eyeless in Gaza at the mill with slaves

carries with it the experience of his own blindness, and of his own disappointed hopes at the passing of the Commonwealth order and the rule of the Saints (the poem was published in 1671). This is perhaps a new feature of the depiction of the Jew in literature made possible by the *personal* religion of the Reformation. We see not merely the Jew as hero but the possibility of expressing through him the personal aspirations, ideals, and values of the author. This will continue in the Romantic period and for such modern writers as George Eliot and James Joyce. It is characteristic of the religion of the seventeenth century that England should as a whole be identified with Israel. This was already noticeable in the sixteenth century when we find Lyly speaking of God's special care for England " as of a new Israel, his chosen and peculiar people." He maintains that " the living God is only the English God." The England/Israel analogy was the chief point of departure for all seventeenth century sermons based on the historical texts of the Old Testament. It could be used either for purposes of praise or rebuke. Thus, to take an example from Joseph Hall, we find him declaring in one sermon : " if any nation under heaven, could either parallel or second Israel in the favour of God, this poor little island of ours is it "; and in another sermon : " I would easily tire you with the odious parallels of our sins with Israel's " (Sermons vi and xl). But this analogy is most vigorously pressed in the era of the Puritan Revolution. Cromwell sees himself as one of the heroes of Biblical antiquity, and so for that matter does Charles I. The Puritan soldiers sing the songs of David when going into battle and apply the contents to their own circumstances. Their enemies the Cavaliers become automatically the Philistines, which helps to explain the *dramatis personae* in Milton's poem.

This gearing of the nation to a messianic destiny had as its corollary a heightened self-awareness on the part of the poet to whom the vision of a new heaven and a new earth had been vouchsafed. For Milton, poets are " the selected heralds of peace, and dispensers of treasure inestimable." Nor should such egotism be regarded as a weakness. Coleridge said of Milton that " the egotism of such a man is a revelation of spirit." Such sublime egotism on the part of poets first appears in the Puritan era and later reappears in the Romantic period. For Shelley too the poet was " the hierophant of an unapprehended inspiration." It is significant that Milton should have found his most satisfying model and channel for self-expression in the career of the Nazirite, Samson. Through the faith of the Israelite, Milton finds the perfect summary of what he regards as his own religious calling, and that perfect combination of Goodness and Power which all poetry and drama implicitly seek, but which is so rarely achieved in either literature or life:

> My trust is in the living God, who gave me,
> At my nativity, this strength, diffused
> No less through all my sinews, joints, and bones,
> Than thine, while I preserve these locks unshorn,
> The pledge of my unviolated vow.

The Eighteenth Century

As we move into the supposedly rational eighteenth century, the portrayal of the Jew does not seem to undergo any immediate process of rationalisation. In Defoe's novel, *Roxana,* the Jew is still represented by the grotesque gesticulating figure made familiar to us in the medieval

Mystery plays. He " put himself into a thousand shapes,
twisting his body, and wringing up his face this way and
that way in his discourse; stamping with his feet, and
throwing abroad his hands, as if he was not in a rage only,
but in a mere fury." His treatment in the novel is of a piece
with this last quotation. In Smollett's *Roderick Random*
(1748) Isaac Rapine is the " old cent-per-cent. fornicator."
Later, in *The Adventures of Count Fathom* (1753), Smollett
presented the opposite image, namely of an amazingly
benevolent Jew, Joshua Manasseh, who agrees to advance
the hero the sum he requires without interest, and makes
a regular practice of such benevolence among Jews and
Gentiles. As M. F. Modder remarks, " It is evident that
in creating Manasseh, Smollett has exaggerated the Jew's
munificence to a ludicrous extreme. Manasseh is just as
impossible as a sentimentally good Jew, as Isaac Rapine
is impossible as an avaricious villain of a Jew." Here is
a good example of the dual image with the good Jews
dressed up very much like good Whig men of feeling. The
immoral aspect of the bad Jew, Isaac, in *Roderick Random* evidently owed something to the portrayal of the
Jew as a whoremonger in Hogarth's series of paintings,
The Harlot's Progress (1733). The quality of licentious-
ness is henceforward added as a spicing for the broth of
literary anti-semitism. It will come up again in Philip Roth
in our own time.

For a more factual and objective account we may turn
to the new periodical essayists. Addison frequently writes
understandingly of the Jews' position in the economic and
social scheme, and informative articles on the Jews appear
from time to time in *The Gentleman's Magazine* during
the first-half of the eighteenth century. One important
difference in the treatment of the Jews in literature during
the eighteenth century is that very often there are touches
of realism and fact derived from the observation of actual
Jews, usually of Spanish and Portuguese origin, in and
about London. (Pepys in his *Diary* anticipated such realism). Jews are themselves becoming prominent in the

national life in one way and another in this period. A Jew such as Sampson Gideon helped his country in the financial crisis of 1754. Later in the century, a Jew, Daniel Mendoza, made himself a legendary fame through his exploits as a prize-fighter. Not all Jews brought glory on their people —the editor of the first translation of the Hebrew Prayer Book, in 1738, one Abraham Mears (pseud. Gamaliel ben Pedahzur) was an apostate Jew who clearly designed through his translation and commentary to bring his people into contempt.

The self-contemptuous assimilationist Jew with many traits drawn from real life now becomes a character in literature and we find a good example early on in Sheridan's comic opera, *The Duenna* (1775). Naturally the Jew who has lost his self-respect comes to reinforce the black or ugly portrait of the Jew of antique legend. In this play, Isaac Mendoza " has left his old religion for an estate and has not had time to get a new one." His lineage from Shylock and Barabas is indicated in the comment of Don Ferdinand that " the most remarkable part of his character is his passion for deceit and tricks of cunning " (Act I, scene iii). The story tells of how his cunning is overreached by the two young gallants of the play, and he is tricked into wedding the old and ugly Duenna (or Governess) of a wealthy family of Seville, thinking her to be the daughter of the household and the heiress of its fortunes. The love scene between the Duenna and Isaac is grotesquely funny; both are made to look as ugly and unattractive as possible whilst they pay one another handsome compliments and make amorous speeches, he to gain a fortune, and she to gain a husband at all costs. In order to heighten the farce, the Duenna takes the initiative and praises him for his liberal carriage, his penetrating eye, and bewitching smile; but what finally wins him is the remark: " So little like a Jew, and so much like a gentleman! "—a remark calculated of course to mollify the heart of the new " enlightened " Jew seeking to establish himself in gentile society. Sheridan balances the portrait (just as Smollett had done) two years later in *The School for Scandal* where he presents, not indeed a good Jew, but a reasonably straightforward Jewish broker, Moses, an " honest Israelite ", who whilst introducing Sir Oliver Surface to the tricks of the usurer's trade, at the same time helps the old gentleman to reclaim his nephew Charles Surface from folly and dissipation. He is to that extent on the side of the angels. In 1785 we find a much more positive representation of the Jewish usurer as a man of feeling and benevolence in the anonymous play, *The Israelites,* or *The Pampered Nabob.* Therein the hero, significantly named, Mr. Israel, declares " I will show you there are some Jews who practise what many Christians only profess." The play made no great impression.

We have now to consider one play in which the Jew plays the principal *rôle*. It is *The Jew*, a comedy by Richard Cumberland, first produced in 1794. It had a fairly remarkable success on the stage, surviving longer than any other sentimental comedy of its period, and it has even been revived occasionally in our own century. Cumberland's attitude to the Jews was almost as ambiguous as that of Smollett or Sheridan. He too had his bad Jew, Naphtali, who figured in an earlier play, *The Fashionable Lover* (1772), but by the time we come to *The Jew* in 1794, the position has altered. He has conceived a plan of presenting a new kind of Jew on the stage, a sort of Shylock in reverse, the Jewish broker superficially resembling the cringing, mean, and unprepossessing figure of tradition but expounded afresh according to the new doctrine of human perfectibility (Godwin's *Enquiry Concerning Political Justice* had been published in the previous year), and the new sentiment of universal tolerance associated with the era of the French Revolution.

When he came to write *The Jew,* Cumberland had a fairly clear and well worked out intention and a theme of considerable dramatic interest involving as its background the new Jewish community in and around Duke's Place, and its impact upon the gentile environment of upper-middle class London society. His aim, as expressed earlier on in journalistic form in *The Observer,* was the rectification through direct human contact of traditional racial animosities. The central character is the Jewish miser and usurer, Sheva, whose relationship with his servant Jabal is at first sight exactly that of Shylock and Launcelot (except that Jabal is himself a Jew). Jabal too complains of the scarcity of food in his master's house. Indeed the close resemblance of the early scenes in dramatic planning to the early scenes of *The Merchant of Venice* is patent. It testifies to the archetypal value of Shakespeare's portrayal of the relationship between Jew and Christian and of the tensions set up between them, and it also shows that Cumberland is deliberately drawing upon his audience's recollection of Shakespeare's play in order to provide a sort of antidote to it. Charles, one of the two young heroes of the play is like Bassanio—in need of the Jew's money in order to meet his obligations and enable himself to marry. His friend Frederic decides to stand surety for him, bidding Sheva, " be ready with your instruments, I care not what they are: only let me have the money, and you may proceed to dissection as soon after as you please ". Clearly he expects to suffer an ordeal similar to that of Antonio, and the audience is settling down comfortably to a new exposure of the stereotyped Jewish villain in the person of Sheva, " the meerest muck-worm in the city of London." But before the end of Act I, we are beginning to doubt whether in fact Sheva is the man to concoct a merciless plot of extortion. He is, first of all, that thing which the late eighteenth century loved so well, a man of sentiment, with tears for all occasions, and a generous sense of human suffering and want. This aspect of his character may not have worn so well in the passing of the Age of Sentiment, but his other, even more attractive quality is his sturdy pride in his people. When Charles praises him by saying " I'll call you Christian then, and this proud merchant [*i.e.,* Frederic's father] Jew," Sheva is not impressed: " I shall not thank you for that compli-

ment "—which is sufficiently unlike the attitude of Isaac
Mendoza in Sheridan's *The Duenna,* who was only too
happy to be called " a gentleman and no Jew." Sheva
goes further. He delivers the two young Christian men a
lecture on the evils of anti-semitism, which is also aimed
at correcting the anti-semitic prejudice of the theatre-going
public of the day:

> If your play-writers want a butt or a buffoon, or a knave to
> make sport of, out comes a Jew to be baited and buffeted
> through five long acts for the amusement of all good
> Christians—Cruel sport, merciless amusement! hard deal-
> ings for a poor stray sheep of the scatter'd flock of Abraham!
> How can you expect us to shew kindness, when we receive
> none?

The speech echoes Shylock's " Hath not a Jew eyes? ",
especially at its climax, " if you wrong us shall we not
revenge? "; but whereas the Shylock of that speech co-
exists with the bloodthirsty Shylock who seeks the life of
the good Christian merchant, Sheva turns out to harbour
no such ambiguities. He is not merely a man with human
feelings and reactions; he is a saint ready to deprive himself of all bodily comforts for the sake of others. His secret
benefactions know no limits, and he saves the situation
for the lovers by settling ten thousand pounds in good
investments upon the distressed couple, even before he
discovers that Eliza is the daughter of his own erstwhile
rescuer from the horrors of the Inquisition! The shock
of the discovery of Sheva in this new character is almost
too much for Sir Stephen, Frederic's rather cantankerous
and crochety father, and it is also, we may suspect, a little
too much for the audience. After this shock treatment
which is intended to dislodge the traditional Shylock from
the public imagination for good and all, the play is carried
forward on a flood of sentimental benevolence. Even
Jabal changes and we are made to realise that he was
only joking in his earlier complaints against his master.
He comes now to Sheva's defence: " Dam it! do you think
I wou'd stand by and hear my master abus'd? "

By the end of the play, Sheva is not merely rehabilitated; he is set far above our normal experience as a devotee of the religion of benevolence:

> *Charles.* This is the man—My benefactor; your's Eliza; Frederics; your's dear mother; all mankind's: The widow's friend, the orphan's father, the poor man's protector, the universal philanthropist.

—and Charles proceeds to demand a change of heart on the part of his fellow Christians " towards your whole nation." From a dramatic point of view, it is easy to see that this sort of characterisation simply does not come off. The tone of the play, it is true, is preserved from complete sentimentality by the comic scenes involving Jabal and Dorcas (Sheva's maidservant) but otherwise the Jew is exposed to laughter on the score of incredibility and inadequate motivation. It is possible to have a melodramatic character of incredible benevolence, just as it is possible to have a melodrama of incredible villainy. Both will inspire laughter in an audience which demands something better than melodrama.

The trouble with Sheva is not that such a Jew is too good, but that he is not distinctively Jewish; his goodness is somehow suspended in a void. It is not drawn from history or psychology but rather from the region of sentimental fantasies. Jews as good as Sheva have surely existed, but their benevolence is part of a complex human reality which has to be portrayed, rather than an isolated, ideal phenomenon. Sheva's goodness does not form a piece with his concrete existence as Ghetto Jew: it is an issue of the *generalised* sentiment of the age rather than of the *particular* facts of Jewish history and Jewish ethics. Much as one would like to claim so good a man for Judaism, the fact is that there is little to identify Sheva as a Jew except his superficial manner, and his habits of dress and speech (the latter sometimes lapsing unaccountably in the direction of standard English). He is a neutral and colourless portrait.

Cumberland was not alone in setting forth the Jew in the new favourable colours of the Age of Enlightenment. In Germany, Lessing's *Nathan der Weise* (1779) had offered an equally favourable, and dramatically more balanced and convincing portrait of the Jew, and this play, which appeared some years before Cumberland's work in English, had possibly influenced Cumberland and encouraged him to visualise the Jew along liberal lines. Now that the age of liberalism has unfortunately passed away, we can see that human nature is not changed by merely preaching a sermon on tolerance, and that simply to lay it down that all men are naturally alike does not make them so. The assumption common at the time that differences of race and tradition are only skin deep does not hold in the light of modern history and the modern science of anthropology. It is interesting to note that Cumberland tried to dissipate anti-Irish prejudice in his play, *The West Indian* (1771). It was also fashionable to stress the extraordinary goodness of the noble savage (a sentimental stock character of the century) in this period and the essential superficiality of his differences from the white man. How oddly this sounds now in the age of Eldridge Cleaver and the Black Power movement!

We would be wrong to underestimate the strength of the idealism which lay behind this movement of tolerance and enlightenment, a movement which was to issue in the great liberal revolutions of the nineteenth century. To such impulses are to be traced the liberation of the slaves, and, as far as Jewry is concerned, the breaking down of the ghetto walls and the widespread emancipation of Jews throughout Western Europe. But the liberal movement— like the literature which it inspired—failed to attack the real roots of anti-semitism. Sheva did not displace Shylock from the stage and, in spite of the wisdom of Nathan, the twentieth century Jew has all too often heard the *hep! hep!* of the German mob with its subconscious undertones of numinous fear and ancestral father-hatred. Shylock and Nathan walk the stage together: in Germany they were very often successfully portrayed by the same actors (notably by Bassermann and Schildkraut). That this paradoxical situation exists is due not only to the failure of the world's great dramatists to reveal the character of the Jew as a person, but also to their failure to comprehend the special vocation and status of Israel among the nations.

CHAPTER THREE

THE ROMANTIC MOVEMENT AND BEYOND

The Poets

The Romantic Movement continued much of the inspiration of late eighteenth century benevolence and tolerance. Wordsworth had felt the thrill of the French Revolution and had responded to the new climate of universal brotherhood. It is not surprising therefore that his poems of humble folk, celebrating the sanctities of hearth and home, should have included one or two of Jewish interest. His *A Jewish Family* (1828) is a descriptive lyric in which the dark-brown curls of the Jewish child more or less exhaust the specifically Jewish character of the poem. His conclusion expresses a certain veneration for the unseen Guardian who has preserved Israel through history:

> Mysterious safeguard, that, in spite
>> Of poverty and wrong,
> Doth here preserve a living light,
>> From Hebrew fountains sprung;
> That gives this ragged group to cast
>> Around the dell a gleam
> Of Palestine, of glory past,
>> And proud Jerusalem!

But we should remind ourselves of a new kind of literary anti-semitism which arose as a by-product of the Enlightenment. (Among Jews also at this period and later the literary movement of Enlightenment (*Haskalah*) produced a strong anti-religious reaction.) We find in Blake as in Voltaire a hatred of the God of the Old Testament as the author of the moral law. In Blake's *Everlasting Gospel* (approx. 1818), the true Jesus is the protagonist of free-love who " lays his hand on Moses' law " and defies the God of Sinai by " putting back the bloody shrine " wherein his moral restrictions are inscribed. This mood is also exemplified by Shelley. In his early poem *Queen Mab* (1813), the free progress of mankind towards the possession of knowledge, love, and beauty in their ideal manifestations are shown to be impeded by the decrees of " tyrannous omnipotence " and his servant Moses whose history is characterised as follows:

> A Murderer heard
> His voice in Egypt, one whose gifts and arts
> Had raised him to his eminence in power,
> Accomplice of omnipotence in crime,
> And confidant of the all-knowing one.

And later, in Shelley's most mature verse-drama, *Prometheus Unbound*, the tyrant-god and enemy of the human race is Jupiter, who reveals no slight imaginative connexion with the God of the Hebrews. Clearly this ideological anti-semitism springs not so much out of a direct reaction to Jews or Judaism as out of the current revolt against evangelical orthodoxy and its negative *Christian* ethic, and also in particular it arose from the Romantic poets' hatred of the ugliness and illiberalism of the Industrial Revolution which was felt (rightly) to be associated with the religion of the non-conformist Middle Classes. This moral revolt in Blake and Shelley is thus in origin a Christian affair; it takes on an anti-semitic character through the false identification of Pauline Christianity—at war always with the World, the Flesh and the Devil—with Hebraism! (Matthew Arnold was later on guilty of the same false identification.) That anti-semitism should be produced as an extension of, and substitute for, anti-Christianity and, in particular, anti-Puritanism, is another example of that unfortunate confusion of values which we are constantly encountering in our discussion of this subject.

In Shelley's case confusion is made more confounded by the fact that in the very poem in which he first issues his defiance to the God of Israel, *viz.*, *Queen Mab*, he also introduces as perhaps the most positive character in the poem, a character no other than Ahasuerus, the Wandering Jew. It is he who, as the author's mouthpiece, expresses the above-quoted blasphemies against the Old Testament God. Yet in contrast to the Wandering Jew as he figures in the ballads, there is here in Shelley no trace of anti-semitic feeling attaching to the Jew himself: he is rather a symbol of endurance " peaceful, and serene, and self-enshrined."

There is no doubt that the Wandering Jew exercised a peculiar compulsion over the romantic imagination. Both Wordsworth and Shelley were deeply impressed by the legend (though Wordsworth's *Song* for the Wandering Jew could equally well have been a song for the Wandering Indian or even for the Leech-gatherer). Shelley treated the subject five times. In his dramatic poem *Hellas,* Ahasuerus appears to reveal to Mahmud the secrets of the past and future:

> What has thought
> To do with time, or place, or circumstance,
> Wouldst thou behold the future? ask and have!
> Knock and it shall be opened—look, and lo!
> The coming age is shadowed on the past
> As on a glass.

Ahasuerus has insight into those truths which remain unchanged in a world of mutability. This positive approach to the legendary Ahasuerus is, however, only made possible by the weakening of the hold of Christian dogma which had earlier served to emphasise the disagreeable traits of the Wandering Jew. Thus we see how the processes of the Enlightenment served at the same time to promote a higher anti-semitism and to make possible a noble and tragic portrayal of the Jew of legend! The interest of the Ahasuerus story for Shelley and Wordsworth had nothing to do with its earlier use as an expression of Christian apologetics: indeed, insofar as the Wandering Jew was a recipient of the Divine curse, he was a figure to be pitied and admired. One could go further and say that the poets tended to identify themselves with the awesome and tragic figure of the Jew: this was especially the case with Shelley, who was an outcast, or at least a voluntary exile, and a rebel against the existing order. The romantic poet liked to think of himself as " a man of sorrows " elected for peculiar privilege and peculiar sufferings, and in the Wandering Jew he found the true model for such a self-portrait.

Coleridge's celebrated poem *The Ancient Mariner*, provides another example of the influence of the Wandering Jew story. There is good evidence that many touches in the mariner's guilt, his expiation, and his extraordinary sub-reading of the legend in M. G. Lewis's fantastic novel *The Monk* (1796) where the Wandering Jew specializes in exorcism and the uncovering of guilty secrets. The mariner's guilt, his expiation, and his extraordinary sub-sequent relation to society as well as the extent of his travels and his experience of life, all are features belonging to the legend; at the same time they reflect the peculiar burdens, obsessions, and intensities of the *poète maudit* of later romanticism.

All this suggests that the romantic poets were interested in Ahasuerus as a projection of themselves rather than in bestowing upon him a distinctive Jewish conscience or colouring. On the other hand, he does signify for them something which belongs essentially to the *rôle* of the Jew among the nations—he signifies the historical conscious-ness and memory of Man. The Jew, bringing with him, as it were about his person, the records and recollections of antiquity, is the supreme symbol of race-memory. He walks through history from the beginning to the end: he endures whilst the nations come and go, and therefore he stirs both awe and terror in the beholder. Part of the terror which the Jew inspires is due to the ancestral guilt which the beholder seek to hide from himself and which the Jew as it were inevitably brings back to remembrance. In the medieval period, that very guilt is transferred by subsitution to the Wandering Jew himself: but the awe remains, investing the figure of Ahasuerus with sombre dignity.

In the late nineteenth century, Robert Buchanan wrote a poem of *The Wandering Jew,* which completely reverses the tradition. In it, the Jew is identified with the Christian Messiah still trying to save the world—but failing because the world's sinfulness, evidenced by its maltreatment of the Jew, is still too great. This comes near to the underlying psychological motive behind the medieval legend.

A more Hebraic tone than Shelley achieves and a more direct delineation of the Jew in history is introduced in Byron's *Hebrew Melodies.* Again the approach to the Jew is positive, even enthusiastically positive. Byron's Biblical drama *Cain,* whilst raising moral issues which one might suspect belong more to Byron's personal history than to an exegesis of the book of *Genesis,* likewise bespeaks a keen and vivid sense of the dramatic power of the Hebrew oracles. The Cain figure also, as G. K. Anderson has shown, embodies many features of the Wandering Jew. Both Cain and the Wandering Jew (in Lewis's *The Monk,* for instance) bear a mark on their forehead. Byron is here again seeking to exhibit his Romantic sense of guilt. The Jew is seen—like the poet—to bear both curse and blessing. But the brighter side of romanticism is also, for Byron, to be found in the Jew. He finds in him a national pride and a love of freedom with which he readily sympathizes. Had the issue of a Jewish national renaissance arisen in his day, we may be sure he would have sacrificed himself as readily for it as he did in the cause of Greek independence.

It seems that the new spirit of tolerance, combined with a general weakening of Christian orthodoxy as a compelling force in poetry, resulted in a presentation of the Jew in poetry which had all the compassion we noticed in Herbert and Vaughan in the seventeenth century but none of their theological questionings and rebukes. Byron's well-known stanza exemplifies the romantic poet's feeling for those who suffer from man's inhumanity to man:

> Tribes of the wandering foot and weary breast,
> How shall ye flee away and be at rest!
> The wild-dove hath her nest, the fox his cave,
> Mankind their country—Israel but the grave!

There is no difficulty now in the poet's identifying himself with suffering Israel, for he is not troubled by any conflicting loyalty. Indeed the romantic poet is himself in revolt against the constricting and stultifying forces (as he conceives them) of Christian morality and Christian institutions, and the Jew may become for him a symbol of a more liberal spirituality, and the Hebraism of the Old Testament may become on some occasions a source of moral and literary inspiration more human and realistic than the austere creed of Puritanism could afford. A line may be traced from Bishop Lowth's *Lectures on the Sacred Poetry of the Hebrews* (1753), through Bishop Percy's prose translation of the *Song of Songs* (1764), to Blake's *Jerusalem* (1804) and Byron's *Hebrew Melodies* (1815).

Browning, later in the nineteenth century, does not find his inspiration in the Old Testament, but he can find no better mouthpiece for his own liberal this-worldly, life-affirming ethical philosophy than the medieval Rabbi Ben Ezra (R. Abraham Ibn Ezra, 1093-1167). His acute understanding of human nature, and his psychological interests, lead him to sympathise with odd people in odd situations. In *Holy Cross Day,* he imagines what the Jews really said to one another when they were driven to Church to hear a compulsory sermon in Rome. The poem reveals a certain insight into Jewish psychology: but more than that it reveals a sardonic humour, and a satirical enjoyment of the hypocrisies of the Roman Catholic hierarchy. But this comic vein gives way at the end to a sombre note of religious meditation and hope, in what he calls " Ben Ezra's Song of Death ":

> The Lord will have mercy on Jacob yet,
> And again in his border see Israel set.
> When Judah beholds Jerusalem,
> The stranger-seed shall be joined to them:
> To Jacob's House shall the Gentiles cleave.
> So the prophet saith and his sons believe.

Examples of sympathetic treatments of Jewish types and of a sympathetic handling of the Jewish problem can be multiplied from the minor poetry of the nineteenth century. But we should remind ourselves that the romantic poets and their followers represented, not the practical sentiment of the century, so much as the fine flower of its idealism. They spoke and sang as the heralds of truths which mankind had not yet achieved and (so the poet sometimes hints) of truths never likely to be achieved. For the poet in his own private world the Messiah has already come and the lion may forthwith lie down with the lamb. But as far as the social order is concerned, the ugliness of the Industrial Revolution and the desperate poverty and inhumanity which it brought in its wake suggest a world in which romantic sentiment has very little part to play. The poet with his sense of compassion, and his sense of beauty both in nature and in human relationships, is henceforward something of an outcast and exile from "the darkling plain" where as Matthew Arnold said, "ignorant armies clash by night." And because he is fundamentally an exile and outcast he sympathises with the nation of exiles and outcasts—the Jews. But in the world of hard realities, of hatreds, of new and old antagonisms, the bright flower of romantic love and sentiment blooms rarely, and for this harsher world it is the novelist rather than the poet who speaks.

The Novelists

Our attention is first drawn to Scott's *Ivanhoe* (1819) as the first full-length treatment of the Jewish character in nineteenth century English fiction. Scott was himself a

romantic poet, and much of the sentiment of benevolence
as well as the idealism which we have noted in the previous
chapter clings to his picture of Isaac of York and his
daughter Rebecca. Scott's medieval tale is a serious effort
to visualise the Jew in medieval society and to combat as
soberly as possible the prejudices he there aroused. But
Scott tries to preserve a balance, and whilst attributing the
disagreeable aspects of the Jewish character to the effects
of Christian oppression, he nevertheless gives considerable
weight to them in his description of Isaac:

> Introduced with little ceremony, and advancing with fear
> and hesitation, and many a bow of deep humility, a tall
> thin old man, who, however, had lost by the habit of stoop-
> ing much of his actual height, approached the lower end of
> the board. His features, keen and regular, with an aquiline
> nose, and piercing black eyes ; his high and wrinkled fore-
> head, and long grey hair and beard, would have been con-
> sidered as handsome, had they not been the marks of a
> physiognomy peculiar to a race, which during those dark
> ages, was alike detested by the credulous and prejudiced
> vulgar, and persecuted by the greedy and rapacious nobility,
> and who, perhaps, owing to that very hatred and persecu-
> tion, had adopted a national character, in which there was
> much, to say the least, mean and unamiable.

Isaac is a usurer, and the various epigraphs to the chapters
in which he appears indicate his lineage from Shylock.
But Scott's enlightened understanding forbids him to see
Isaac at any time as a bloodthirsty villain: a materialist
and coward, yes, but a villain, no. Scott's picture of the
medieval usurer is, in short, humanised to the point of
making him, if not a sympathetic picture, at any rate an
understandable one.

With Isaac's daughter Rebecca it is different. On her
the author lavishes all the beauty and goodness which his
romantic imagination could conceive. We note again the
black and white, or at any rate, grey and white, contrast
between the Jew and his daughter, as in Shakespeare.
Rebecca is the true heroine of the novel, endearing herself
to the reader even more than the nominal heroine Rowena,

because, as a Jewess, she has to suffer from undeserved discrimination. The hero, Ivanhoe, rescues her from death, but the reader is deprived of the normal romantic ending in which the beautiful lady and her rescuer proceed to nuptualities, because of the insurmountable racial and religious barriers between them. Her sad plight as the beatiful and tragically lonely Jewess is sufficient to arouse the tender emotions, but she is also meant to inspire admiration and respect through her wisdom and her well-aimed criticism of medieval society. In her speeches, the novelist voices his opinions on the bloodthirstiness of the tourney and the moral emptiness of the code of chivalry as a whole. The Jew may be unduly preoccupied with money but he no longer carries blood-guiltiness; that is squarely placed to the account of the Jew's enemies. Nor indeed is Israel in its historical ancestry and origin a nation of misers and usurers. In her final debate with her would-be seducer, the villainous Knight Templar, Bois-Guilbert, Rebecca eloquently and proudly describes the past glories of her people (in this of course very unlike the apostate type of good Jewess in Marlowe and Shakespeare) and recommends the knight to read in the Old Testament of the ancient Israelite stock of noblemen and heroes:

> Such were the princes of Judah, now such no more!—They are trampled down like the shorn grass, and mixed with the mire of the ways. Yet there are those among them who shame not such high descent, and of such shall be the daughter of Isaac the son of Adonikam! Farewell! I envy not thy blood-won honours—I envy not thy barbarous descent from northern heathens—I envy thee not thy faith, which is ever in thy mouth, but never in thy heart nor in thy practice.

That is the high water-mark of moral passion as expressed in this novel, and it is significant that such idealistic utterances are given to the Jewess rather than to any other character.

It is notable that the Jew is here used to shoot the arrows of bourgeois realism and bourgeois morality against the false values of the aristocracy. This is the inner meaning of the debate between Rebecca and Bois-Guilbert. In a sense this is already anticipated in Shakespeare who sets off Shylock and his world against the tinsel landscape of Belmont. The novel as it developed in the seventeenth and eighteenth centuries developed this confrontation as a major theme. For the novel was the literary medium of the rising middle class. Rebecca has the same lesson to teach Bois-Guilbert as Fanny has for the impudent Squire Didapper in Fielding's *Joseph Andrews*. The Jew with his sturdy respectability and family loyalty has become the hero of a middle class fable. And this aspect will reappear again in numerous authors down to E. M. Forster and C. P. Snow in our own century.

The mere fact that the Jew has become the hero of a realistic work of fiction is significant. In the Middle Ages such Jewish characters are represented only by the Israelites of Old Testament antiquity: from Judas onward it is felt that the character of the Jew has somehow radically changed for the worse—that is, unless he adopts Christianity. The fact that favourable, even ecstatically favourable, portraits of *post-Biblical* Jews can now appear in literature shows that this theological distinction has now no meaning for the romantic writer. But that does not mean that the dual image has been abolished. It is simply that the dividing line has shifted. There is Rebecca, but there is also Isaac. Earlier on, Maria Edgeworth had produced two contrasting types, the bad Jew Mordecai in *The Absentee* (1812) and the white Jew Mr. Montenero in *Harrington* (1817).

Scott, towards the end of his life, drew a further set of Jewish characters in *The Surgeon's Daughter* (1827). These are far less sympathetic than the Jews of *Ivanhoe*. Richard Middlemas, the half-Jewish rogue, is in particular ambitious, violent, and treacherous. The novel ends somewhat extravagantly with Richard being crushed to death by an elephant in India.

In realistic fiction, the Jew is more likely to be a figure of evil than a figure of good. We may instance Charles

Kingsley's *Alton Locke* (1850) in which Jews are mentioned exclusively in connexion with the evils of the new sweat-shops in the tailoring industry. Thackeray very often turns his attention (in a rather incidental way) to Jews, and invariably treats them to a little pleasant sarcasm on the score of their supposed deceits and malpractices. His keen powers of social satire likewise find an easy target in the *nouveau riche* type of Jew trying to get on in gentile society. Such references in his novels tend to be merely incidental: in his journalistic work, as for instance in his account of his trip to Palestine (*From Cornhill to Cairo*, 1846), he reveals a more vicious strain of anti-semitism.

The most celebrated treatment of the Jew in Victorian fiction is of course to be found in Dickens. In the character of Fagin, the receiver of stolen goods, as presented in *Oliver Twist* (1837-8), Dickens has given a caricature portrait of the evil Jew of legend. The medieval details are curiously correct: his red hair, his blasphemies, his penchant for drugs and poisoning, his blood-guiltiness, and his grotesque humour. But the figure is secularised. He is not the enemy of Christianity, so much as the enemy of all good folk with kindly souls. He is simply the villain writ large, and more disagreeable even than Bill Sykes because his villainy is of the cunning and calculating kind rather than simply a matter of brutishness. Fagin is always "The Jew," and Dickens is here clearly not so much exploring a contemporary type as working on a stock figure associated in the public imagination with the word ' Jew.' Thus his character of Fagin testifies to the continuing vitality of the Judas-Devil myth in spite of the new liberal atmosphere which, as it happens, Dickens himself in other respects helped so much to diffuse.

Dickens was rebuked by a Jewish lady, Mrs. Eliza Davis for his injustice to the Jewish race in *Oliver Twist*, and perhaps this prompted him to balance the portrait some years later in *Our Mutual Friend* (1864-5). There he gives us Mr. Riah, the Jewish agent, who is as good and well-meaning as Fagin was crafty and villainous. Fascination

Fledgeby, Riah's gentile employer, is now the crafty unscrupulous and avaricious wretch of the Fagin type! The
rôles have been exactly reversed :

"Now, you sir!" cried Fledgeby. "These are nice
games!"

He addressed an old Jewish man in an ancient coat, long
of skirt, and wide of pocket. A venerable man, bald and
shining at the top of his head, and with long grey hair
flowing down at its sides and mingling with his beard. A
man who, with a graceful Eastern action of homage, bent
his head and stretched out his hands with the palms down-
wards, as if to deprecate the wrath of a superior.

"What have you been up to?" said Fledgeby, storming
at him.

"Generous Christian master," urged the Jewish man,
"it being holiday, I looked for no one."

"Holiday be blowed!" said Fledgeby, entering. "What
have you got to do with holidays? Shut the door." . . .

Perched on the stool, with his hat cocked on his head,
and one of his legs dangling, the youth of Fledgeby hardly
contrasted to advantage with the age of the Jewish man as
he stood with his bare head bowed, and his eyes (which he
only raised in speaking) on the ground. His clothing was
worn down to the rusty hue of the hat in the entry, but
though he looked shabby, he did not look mean. Now,
Fledgeby, though not shabby, did look mean.

"You have not told me what you were up to, you sir,"
said Fledgeby, scratching his head with the brim of his hat.

"Sir, I was breathing the air."

"In the cellar, that you didn't hear?"

"On the house-top."

"Upon my soul! That's a way of doing business."

"Sir," the old man represented with a grave and patient
air, "there must be two parties to the transaction of business,
and the holiday has left me alone." . . .

"Your people need speak the truth sometimes, for they
lie enough," remarked Fascination Fledgeby.

"Sir, there is," returned the old man with quiet emphasis,
"too much untruth among all denominations of men."

Rather dashed, Fascination Fledgeby took another scratch
at his intellectual head with his hat, to gain time for
rallying.

"For instance," he resumed, as though it were he who
had spoken last, "who but you and I ever heard of a poor

Jew? "

"The Jews," said the old man, raising his eyes from the ground with his former smile. "They hear of poor Jews often, and are very good to them."

Here then is Dickens's contribution to the formulation of the dual image. He gives us the figure of the Jew who preys upon all good folk, corrupts youth and compasses every sort of crime; and he gives us the Jew who protects the weak and fatherless and humbly submits to calumny and ill-treatment. But in a way both are neutral portraits—they have neither of them much specific Jewish quality. Fagin with few alterations could be interchanged with some other particularly detestable villain in the Dickens canon; Mr. Riah has little to distinguish him from the hundred other kindly old gentlemen in humble occupations invented by the same author. The identification of them as Jews simply gives them extra piquancy by drawing upon a well-established and colourful convention which would help to control the audience's reaction to their characters.

On the whole, the Victorian novelists stick to the stereotyped figure of the Jew. Charles Reade presents as a central character in his novel *It Is Never Too Late to Mend* (1856) a Jew, Isaac Levi, who starts out by being more sinned against than sinning, but ends by taking a terrible revenge on his foe, the rascally John Meadows. Reade's point seems to be, as Rosenberg points out, that " behind every Sheva lurks a Shylock." Anthony Trollope gives us in *The Way We Live Now* (1875) the fantastically wicked Jew Augustus Melmotte drawn on the gigantic scale of melodrama and with no attempt at verisimilitude. But the most grotesquely infamous Jew of all is that of George Du Maurier in *Trilby* (1894). Here the traditional stereotypes are made more sinister by the influence of late nineteenth century philosophies of race. Svengali, the villain of that novel, is the evil Jew of tradition, a mixture of Shylock and the Wandering Jew: he is also the eternal alien, mysterious and dark. Du Maurier makes no claim to realism. He is writing a kind of Gothic thriller in which much of the audience's interest is focused on the occult powers of Svengali. Svengali is a preternatural genius in two senses: first, he has an incredible musical ability, transporting his hearers into heaven with holy raptures; second, he is a mesmerist having occult powers which he exercises over the heroine, Trilby. He is able to convert her very ordinary nondescript voice into that of a night-ingale. But the dominant reaction that he arouses in the audience is that of loathing and fear. He belongs to an inferior race, and his courting of the heroine is evidently intended to symbolize the corruption of the pure white races by the leering and evil Semite.

But nineteenth century theories of race did not always work to the detriment of the Jews. George Eliot (*alias* Mary Ann Evans) wrote her famous last novel *Daniel Deronda* (1875) largely under the impact of the new interest in nationalism and ethnology. Differences of nationality are important and should be respected. Moreover, the acknowledgment of this leads her (as it led Disraeli earlier in the century) to a high estimation of the function of the Jews in the economy of mankind. For her the Jewish nation was by no means inferior to the rest. The opposite was the case. Instead of Svengali, the Jewish oriental, levelling his evil charm against the representative of the purer white races, we have the high-minded Jew, Deronda, seeking to help the erring British maiden, Gwendolen Harleth who, throughout the novel, is suffering rather severe domestic troubles. Deronda also (like Svengali) exercises a kind of mesmeric charm over the English maiden (this is stressed in the first Chapter of *Daniel Deronda*) but there is not the least trace of sexual exploita-tion on the part of Deronda. If anything, it is Gwendolen who allows herself to become attracted to Deronda. She would have liked to marry him, but she must learn by the end of the novel to keep her distance, whilst Deronda devotes himself to the solution of problems far transcend-ing her little sphere.

As a study of the Jewish problem George Eliot's novel does not lack comprehensiveness. She is capable of drawing the unprepossessing Jewish *petit-bourgeois* in the person of Ezra Cohen, who passes from his Friday night sanctities to his pawnbroking business, and drives a hard bargain with Deronda over a diamond ring. But this character of " oily cheerfulness " represents only a marginal example of Jewish psychology—the real duality which confronts the serious students of Jewry is formed by the Jew who accepts and acknowledges his Jewish identity on the one hand, and the Jew who tries to escape from it on the other. The former is, in Sartre's terms, the authentic Jew : the latter is the inauthentic. George Eliot has got near enough to Jewish life to discover this crucial determinant of Jewish character. The inauthentic Jew yields a psychology marked by evasiveness, self-contempt, and weakness; the authentic Jew bears the burden of the exile with a certain pride, nourishes the promises of the past and the hope of the future, and lives his real life inwardly rather than in a vain attempt to " normalize " his status in the gentile world. Deronda who discovers his Jewish parentage in the course of the book is such a person : the discovery leads to new self-respect, new and galvanizing life-aims, and a sense of high purpose shared with the collectivity of Israel. But in the Philosophers' Club, the group of Jews to whom he resorts for enlightenment on matters Jewish, Daniel meets both types of Jews. On the one hand, there is Gideon, who believed in a reformed Judaism (like so many nineteenth century emancipated Jews whom George Eliot would have met). He wanted a faith adapted to a non-Jewish environment with all the stress removed from nationality and exclusiveness:

I'm a rational Jew myself. I stand by my people as a sort of family relations, and I am for keeping up my worship in a rational way. I don't approve of our people being baptised . . . But I am for getting rid of our superstitions and exclusiveness. There's no reason now why we shouldn't melt gradually into the populations we live among.

Mordecai, on the other hand, is the Jewish sage and intellectual, knowing too much of the history and wisdom of Israel to overvalue the benefits of Western liberalism and of the new, shallow rationalism and egalitarianism which had seduced his brethren. He declares:

> Each nation has its own work, and is a member of the world, enriched by the work of each. But it is true, as Jehuda-ha-Levi first said, that Israel is the heart of mankind, if we mean by heart the core of affections which binds a race and its families in dutiful love, and the reverence for the human body which lifts the needs of our animal life into religion. . . . Where else is there a nation of whom it may be as truly said that their religion and law and moral life mingled as the stream in the heart and made one growth . . . ?

Mordecai's religious Zionism, his demand to " Revive the organic centre," gives the book, in its historical context, an oddly prophetic character, but even in the generation before Herzl, Zionist sentiments were in the air (witness the work of Rabbi Zwi Hirsch Kalischer and Moses Hess), and George Eliot's intuition of this was part of her general understanding for contemporary ideological trends shown in her work as a whole. In this case, her book even helped to stimulate the Zionist renaissance through its impact on men like Eliezer ben Yehudah, the restorer of the Hebrew language, as well as on writers such as Peretz Smolenskin. She had shown that she had more than an intelligent sympathy for Jews; she had a real and detailed knowledge of Jewish thought and tradition of a kind unprecedented in Christian writers in this country, at any rate in the field of *belles lettres*. And she sets a high standard in this respect for her successors.

Nevertheless, it should be added that literary critics from Henry James to F. R. Leavis have criticized this novel in comparison with other works of Eliot. They have complained that the whole Zionist part is inflated and rhetorical, and they have focused attention rather on the English upper middle-class characters, Gwendolen and Henleigh Grandcourt, whose domestic drama of tragic misalliance

occupies much of the forefront of attention. This side of
the novel, it is claimed, is marked by a closer attention
to psychological realism and a more minute study of social
manners. Leavis has even suggested cutting out the Zionist
side by a kind of critical surgery and renaming the novel
Gwendolen Harleth!

It is true that there are stylistic and tonal differences
between the two halves of the book, but George Eliot was
herself aware of this and yet claimed very emphatically
that " everything in the book is to be related to everything
else there." She intended the contrast between the English
upper class world and its values on the one hand, and the
world of the Jew carrying his historic burden on the other.
The one is marked by minute observation of manners and
morals, the other by the grander gestures of the epic, by
a more eloquent style and a more Gothic tone. It is the
conjunction of romance and realism that she is aiming it.
The Jew seeking his historical destiny is the Romantic—
she says so in Chapter XLI—whilst Gwendolen weighing
her marriage prospects and making her small social calculations is the heroine of a drama of manners.

> Could there be a slenderer, more insignificant thread in
> human history than this consciousness of a girl, busy with
> her small inferences of the way in which she could make
> her life pleasant?—in a time too when ideas were with
> fresh vigour making armies of themselves, and the universal
> kinship was declaring itself fiercely. (Chapter XI.)

In putting side by side the universal stream of ideas represented by Deronda, and the private *Biedermeier* world of
Gwendolen, and in allowing the two characters to come
together for discussion and mutual aid, Eliot has a definite
purpose. It is to provide an ironical perspective, a contrast.
She is trying to show the limitations of the English upper
middle class. In much the same way, Meredith in *The
Tragic Comedians* (1880) had introduced the romantic
revolutionary figure Alvan (a *persona* for the Jewish
socialist leader Ferdinand Lassalle) into a circle of German

provincial aristocracy. George Eliot and Meredith are trying to show what happens when genius irrupts into provincial decorum, when dramatically and unpredictably,

> After the cups the marmalade, the tea,
> Among the porcelain, among some talk of you and me—

someone appears who dares to disturb the universe and roll it towards some overwhelming question.

Eliot's aim is to create something like Tolstoy's *War and Peace*, where the doings of the characters, their loves and disappointments are set off against the august backdrop of the Napoleonic invasion of Russia. She is seeking to give to the everyday doings of the English middle classes the same Tolstoyan range and depth. She had achieved something like this some years earlier in *Middlemarch* (1871), introducing a St. Theresa figure into an English country town. But Dorothea finally abandons her exalted destiny and relapses into mere provinciality. She hoped to do even better by introducing the Jew as the connecting link between the quotidian and the sublime in *Daniel Deronda*. Eliot had noticed that among the Jews it was possible for the ordinary to co-exist with the extraordinary, the visionary gleam with the materialism of everyday, as in Rembrandt's Jewish portraiture. What she found in the household of Ezra Cohen was a huckster and a prophet (Mordecai) sharing the same roof:

> It was an unaccountable conjunction—the presence among these common prosperous, shopkeeping types, of a man who in emaciated threadbare condition, imposed a certain awe on Deronda. (Chapter XXXIV.)

It was an " unaccountable conjunction " in general, but accountable she hints in terms of the special conditions of Jewish existence. Here messianic zeal can function against a background of the tawdry and the humdrum. George Eliot had an intuition of the peculiar exposure of Jews to world history. The grander movements of ideas, the history of nations is very much her theme. And the Jew is here peculiarly in place, for he lives in the glare of world history: the destiny of nations is his private destiny. He may try to retire from history into some domestic Dutch interior—and no-one knows better than he how to contrive such domesticity—but in the end (as the twentieth century has taught us) history will find him out. The introduction of the Jew into the setting of the English middle class as represented by Grandcourt, Gwendolen, and Mr. Bult thus enabled Eliot to operate with two time-schemes, the time of personal living and the time of nations, of historic epochs, and to somehow relate the two together.

This was her aim. Yet it must be admitted that the attempt does not wholly succeed. The Jewish part of the book is not fully integrated with the rest. To that extent the disjunctive critics are right. Perhaps the basic difficulty is that George Eliot, in spite of her great sympathy with the Jewish characters, is really observing them from the outside, from a standpoint within the Gwendolen-Grandcourt world. She does not achieve a sufficiently massive realization of Jewish experience from within. Her Jewish characters, especially Daniel and Mordecai, take on an etherealized pre-Raphaelite quality which is never wholly dispelled. They do not achieve the same substantiality as Mr. Bult and the Rev. Gascoigne belonging as they do to a circle whom George Eliot knew so much better. Thus the two images never really coincide. The Jew, as so often in history itself, refuses to assimilate and the non-Jew refuses to assimilate him.

The problem of focusing the novel (which is what finally defeats the author) is at bottom the problem of producing a coherent image of the Jew and his relation to the non-Jew. The dual image haunts the novelist's work at the technical level when it has been banished from his consciousness and moral outlook, creating distance where he requires proximity, strangeness where he requires intimacy, shrillness where he requires quiet persuasiveness. And we may suspect that the same dual image will remain—for the non-Jewish writer at any rate—until such time as Jew and gentile have found some common basis from which to view their respective destinies in the world.

The Jewish Contribution

One great and important change which took place in the course of the nineteenth century was that Jews themselves were emerging on the scene as writers of novels and plays, and a considerable Anglo-Jewish reading public had formed itself. One senses that Eliot's *Daniel Deronda* was written very much with an eye for Jewish readers, and perhaps this led to a greater sense of responsibility in the handling of Jewish characters. On the whole, the portrait of the Jew becomes more charitable, for this reason. A conversionist novel such as Charlotte Elizabeth Phelan's *Judah's Lion* (1843), breathes a strain of love and admiration for Jewry and preaches Israel regenerate and revived upon his own soil:

> I speak of Israel as a nation, now a sapless trunk indeed, blighted and naked, and to all appearance dead: but for the sake of the root, which was holy before God, he will once more cause life to circulate, and the old tree to put forth leaves and branches yet again: ay, and such branches too shall overshadow the whole earth.

Here is once again the parable of the good olive tree as in George Herbert's poem, *The Jews,* and in this novel too the chief Jewish characters are eventually converted to Christianity so ushering in the dawn of a new and blissful era for mankind. The novel is, from a literary point of view, not particularly important but shows a certain interest in contemporary Jewry and in the Jewish political future in the Holy Land.

The most illustrious Jewish convert to Christianity in the nineteenth century, Benjamin Disraeli, also wrote novels in which both the People and the Land of Israel figure, but they never seem to carry that powerful Christian message that Miss Phelan addressed to her readers. Sometimes one thinks that Disraeli was less interested in converting his Jewish friends to Christianity than in bringing the gentiles to a proper appreciation of Judaism, " What, I convert to Christianity? ", he once said, " Why it is the Gentiles who are converts to Judaism! " His first novel, *David Alroy,* (1832), is an historical extravaganza set in the twelfth century in which the chief characters, Alroy, the legendary descendant of the House of David, and Jabaster, the High Priest, conspire to lead the Jews of Azerbaijan back to Palestine, there to restore the Jewish kingdom. The plan comes to nothing, but Alroy triumphs as a tragic hero by preferring death to apostasy. All Disraeli's novels are autobiographical, and here there is no doubt that he has dreamed himself into the heroism of Alroy on the one hand, and the priestly piety of Jabaster on the other. The novel thus tells us a great deal about Disraeli's subconscious (and perhaps not only subconscious) self-identification with Jewry and Judaism. On the other hand it is not so well informed in matters of Jewish literature and history as, say, George Eliot's *Daniel Deronda,* and his Jewish characters fail to convince as objective portraits.

In his more mature novels, Disraeli constantly reverts to Jews, Jerusalem, and the Jewish question. In *Coningsby* (1844), he gives us the character of Sidonia (again a subjective fantasy), whose superhuman gifts of wisdom and knowledge are placed at the disposal of the hero in his attempts to revitalise English political life:

> Sidonia had exhausted all the sources of human knowledge; he was master of the learning of every nation, of all tongues dead or living, of every literature, Western and Oriental. He had pursued the speculations of science to their last term, and had himself illustrated them by observation and experiment. He had lived in all orders of society, had viewed every combination of Nature and of Art, and had observed man under every phasis of civilisation. He had even studied him in the wilderness. The influence of creeds and laws, manners, customs, traditions, in all their

diversities, had been subjected to his personal scrutiny . . .

One source of interest Sidonia found in his descent and in the fortunes of his race. As firm in his adherence to the code of the great Legislator as if the trumpet still sounded on Sinai, he might have received in the conviction of divine favour an adequate compensation for human persecution. But there were other and more terrestrial considerations that made Sidonia proud of his origin, and confident in the future of his kind. Sidonia was a great philosopher, who took comprehensive views of human affairs, and surveyed every fact in its relative position to other facts, the only mode of obtaining truth.

Here is the omnicompetent and omniscient Jew of Disraeli's imagination. He appears again in *Tancred* (1847) guiding in some mysterious way the destinies of Tancred, the hero whose self-appointed task it is to revive the power and influence of the Church of England! There is clearly some psychological confusion here. The form that the dual image takes in Disraeli is a product of the peculiar distortions of his Judeo-Christian mentality. On the one hand, he celebrates Jews like Sidonia, Besso, and Eva (another perfect and beautiful Jewess of the Rebecca-Mirah family whom his hero meets in Jerusalem); on the other hand, his hero is committed to the doctrine of salvation through the universal reign of the Christian King and Saviour. If Disraeli distributed part of himself (or at least part of his imagined self) to Sidonia, he also distributed part of himself to Tancred, the young Anglican apostle, to Contarini Fleming, the outsider trying to get on in an alien environment, and to Vivian Grey, the rather precocious and ineffectual aspirant to fame. On the one hand, Disraeli spends his life in trying to establish himself successfully in the world of British politics by making himself into the most perfect English aristocrat; on the other hand, he makes satirical fun in *Tancred* of the " Mesdemoiselles Laurella " who were " ashamed of their race and not fanatically devoted to their religion " and in the perfect style of the assimilated Jewess of English society, he makes Sophonisbe declare that " the Jews would not be so much disliked if they were better known; that all they had to do was to imitate as closely as possible the habits and customs of the nation among whom they chanced to live . . ." On the one hand, Disraeli constantly declares his belief in the principle of race, maintaining that the Jews were the purest race in the world; and yet his efforts are devoted to the greater glory of England, and of the English Church and Nation as the New Israel destined to govern an Empire in which all the dreams of the prophets of Israel are to be fulfilled! It is no wonder that Disraeli's romantic ideas were received with some uneasiness both by Jew and Gentile. He represents, both in his life and in his work, a peculiar and complex example of the dual image.

However much Disraeli may have been preoccupied by Jews and the Jewish Question (his full-scale treatment of the latter is contained in his *Life of Lord Bentinck,* 1852) his novels were primarily addressed to, and read by, the Great British Public as a whole. Literature more exclusively aimed at the Anglo-Jewish reader becomes more important as the century proceeds. One begins with such a pious and well-intentioned novelist as Grace Aguilar (1816-1847), whose *Characters and Sketches from the Holy Scriptures and Jewish History,* represented the kind of domestic literature of edification for the Anglo-Jewish family in the earlier nineteenth century. A franker and more critical exposition of the life of the Jewish middle-class is provided by Amy Levy, author of *Reuben Sachs* (1889). And by the end of the century, we come upon Israel Zangwill producing a body of work of rich variety and literary significance. His is a unique contribution to Anglo-Jewish letters, and his portrait of the Jew represents a gallery of types of the first importance for the understanding of our subject.

Zangwill achieved that specifically Jewish combination of comedy and pathos which we recognise in Peretz and Sholom Aleichem on the continent. He first appears on the Anglo-Jewish literary scene as a writer of humorous short stories rather in the manner of his friend Jerome K.

Jerome, with a dash of rich caricature reminiscent of Dickens. His *King of Schnorrers* (1894) is a good example of his early style with its truly great comic figure, Manasseh Bueno Barzilai Azavedo da Costa. Laughter is the medium through which we view him, but it is a laughter which holds in solution the two parts of his character; the Schnorrer (professional beggar) with his home-made turban, his grotesque overcoat, his deceits, his sloth, his roguery; and the king, with his pride, his consciousness of his Sephardi superiority his unfailing dignity, his resourcefulness, and his apt quotations from the Talmud. In his meeting with the financier, Grobstock, he is described as "towering above the unhappy capitalist, like an ancient prophet denouncing a swollen monarch"—and the situation that unfolds when Grobstock is caught out by the Schnorrer is richly entertaining. The highlight of the book is reached when we see Manasseh in the synagogue on the Sabbath preceding his daughter's marriage loudly offering great donations to charity to the astonishment of the beholders! The following day we see him visiting the congregants to raise the necessary £100 so as to prevent the synagogue having a bad debt! This contrast between the hero's Sabbath magnificence and his Sunday morning beggary is, in comic form, the version of the dual image which we get in the literature of Jewry itself. The ambiguity is the result of the conditions of life of a Covenant People which is nevertheless cast among the nations to beg a livelihood. Zangwill illustrates this situation by opposed groups of characters; on the one hand we have many staunch self-respecting characters; on the other hand we have the cringing, the broken-spirited, and the vicious. But Zangwill is also capable of illustrating the situation as the double psychological aspect of one and the same character! This is perhaps the subtlest difference between the dual image as it appears to the Jew and as it appears to the non-Jew. The Jew knows that until he has come to terms with his destiny he is an ambiguous figure harbouring within himself strengths and weaknesses, glory and reproach. The dual image is interiorised. On the one hand, there is the centripetal pull of the Covenant demanding loyalty, integrity and an adherence to Jewish spiritual values; on the other hand, there is the centrifugal force of assimilation, weakness, the abandonment of self-respect and the pursuit of purely material or temporal ends. This is the central conflict of all Zangwill's serious writing. It is the theme of his *Children of the Ghetto* (1892), where the important characters are seen to live what he calls " double lives," from the heroine Esther who is torn between life in the ghetto with her pious father and grandmother, and emancipation in the world outside with its secular values—to the Hebrew poet Melchitzedek Pinchas (evidently a rather unflattering caricature of N. H. Imber, author of the Hebrew national anthem *Hatikvah*) who writes lyrics of Zion in the style of Judah Halevi but supplements his income by producing Hebrew propaganda for the missionaries in the East End of London. The same theme may be discovered in practically all the characters described in his *Dreamers of the Ghetto* (1896)—Heine, Lassalle, Disraeli, and others. They too are torn between apostasy and the ghetto forms of life. In *Children of the Ghetto*, the characters generally remained in, or went back to, the ghetto; in *Dreamers of the Ghetto*, they generally chose the road of apostasy; but in both, the essential experiential reality on which this reading of Jewish life is based is the duality itself, the unresolved problem of dual loyalty.

Israel Zangwill in fact could tell us most of what we need to know about our subject, but we must content ourselves here with referring in conclusion to one of his short stories collected under the title of *Ghetto Tragedies* (1899). The story in question is entitled *Diary of a Meshummad* (i.e., Apostate). In it, he portrays the dual attitude of the Jew who is trying to bury his Jewish past, whilst at the same time, he is secretly trying to relive it. We may quote two entries in the diary. Both refer to Jews and Judaism:

The thought of the men, of their gaberdines and their pious ringlets, of their studious dronings and their devout quiverings and wailings, of the women with their coarse figures and their unsightly wigs; the remembrance of their vulgar dialect, and their shuffling ways, and their accommodating morality, filled me with repulsion.

. . . my heart faints within me for the simple, sublime faith of my people. Behind all the tangled network of ceremony and ritual, the larger mind of the man who has lived and loved sees the outlines of a creed grand in its simplicity, sublime in its persistence. The spirit has clothed itself with flesh, as it must do for human eyes to gaze on it and live with it. . .

What makes Zangwill so important a writer is the fundamental seriousness of his writing in relation to Jews and Judaism. In this he is in contrast to Disraeli, for whom one often feels that this subject (like so many others) is no life and death matter. His approach is basically fantastic, whereas for Zangwill the problem of double-lives is his own problem. For him, it is a crisis of identity. A ghetto-Jew himself, he had a strong sense of the values which stemmed from the ghetto, its warmth and vitality. At the same time he was on his way out (he turned from Jewish themes to a great extent later on) intoxicated by the opportunities of the great world. His failure was that he could not rise above his generation and see the possibility of a stable and significant Jewish existence outside the ghetto. But to achieve this, he would have had to achieve, in place of the dual image, a unified image of Jewish life, in which the Jewish past and the Jewish future find real expression in the Jewish present. It is doubtful whether any Jewish writer has ever to date achieved more than a trembling intuition of such a possibility. In general, the *Diaspora* Jew is committed, like his non-Jewish colleague, to a version of the dual image. It is a different version from that of the non-Jewish writer, of course: its negative component is less grotesque; its positive component is less unrealistic and remote from life. But it issues from a similar region of spiritual conflict. The non-

Jewish world, we may say, is in revolt against the Jewish God, and this explains the peculiar virulence of its attack upon His witnesses, namely the Jews. But the non-Jewish world has also inherited the God of the Jews, and cannot wholly escape Him: this dual situation is clearly discernible in the Christian gospels and in the literary examples we have been discussing. But the Jew is likewise placed in an existential dilemma with regard to his obedience to the Jewish God. On the one hand, He is the God of Israel to whom the Jew is bound by love, obedience and by ancestral memories of the most sacred and intimate kind. On the other hand, He is the God who has laid upon the Jew the burden of exile, of the noon-tide arrow, and the terror by night. When the Jew seeks to escape from the awful challenge of Jewish history, he sees in the face of his People and in his own image, not majesty and greatness, but ugliness, pusillanimity, self-contempt, and all the moral and physical ills that flesh is heir to.

CHAPTER FOUR

THE TWENTIETH CENTURY

Liberals and Reactionaries

When we turn to the twentieth century we note that in spite of the generally soberer presentation of Jews the mythological outline remains. In E. M. Forster's early novel, *The Longest Journey* (1907), the Jewish Hegelian philosopher from Cambridge, Stewart Ansell performs a task in relation to the hero Rickie similar to that of Deronda in relation to Gwendolen in George Eliot's novel. He is the cultural and moral catalyst. He exposes the emptiness and triviality of the English upper class, its petty hypocrisies, and serves as a kind of lay-confessor to Rickie who is seeking moral integrity but constantly lapsing into self-deception and weakness. It is Ansell who screws him to the sticking point and forces him, simply through the effect of character and example, to be true to himself. In the great central scene where the accounts are cleared (there is always such a scene in a Forster novel) Ansell occupies the front of the stage : " He seemed transfigured into a Hebrew prophet passionate for satire and truth."

One of Ansell's functions is to be the representative of the honest middle classes—his father is a provincial draper —bringing honesty and realism into the world of the decayed gentry. He also strives to make them appreciate Stephen, the illegitimate half-brother of Rickie who seems to represent the life of the earth, of the proletariat. Ansell's function in the social structure is thus that of a symbolic reconciler of opposites. His message is the same as that

of Margaret Schlegel in *Howard's End* later on (1910)—
" only connect!" It is given to the Jew to achieve both
the necessary detachment and the necessary moral vision
for this purpose.

The place of the Jew in the newly evolving social pattern
is a natural preoccupation of twentieth century writers,
conscious as they are of the disruption of the nineteenth
century class system. This applies also to Galsworthy's
thoughtful and balanced study of the Jew in an alien
society. His *Loyalties* (1922) is a piece of social analysis
in dramatic form rather than a profound work of art, but
its human insight and subtlety of characterisation are
nonetheless impressive. In his study of the *nouveau riche*
Jew, Ferdinand de Levis, trying to establish himself among
the English upper-class, he shows how, in spite of the
gentlemanly tolerance of the English, the Jew in a moment
of crisis is neither a fellow nor an equal, but an outsider
whose presence is a source of wrath and embarrassment,
and whose cause by being just does not cease to be
obnoxious.

The crisis occurs when Ferdinand discovers that a large
sum of money belonging to him has been stolen at a house-
party. His suspicions rightly settle upon a fellow guest,
Captain Ronald Dancy, whose known impecuniosity and
recklessness and certain other circumstances make it
appear probable that he was the thief. The other decent-
minded English folk, however (including General Canynge
and Charles Winsor), are seen to band themselves together
to protect Dancy not because they believe him innocent
but because he is an officer and a gentleman. For them,
Ferdinand's appeal to the law is simply bad form. Other
characters however, such as Adela Winsor, are capable
of weighing the case up impartially and getting beyond
immediate class-loyalties. Eventually the truth comes to
light, when two of the stolen bank notes turn up in the
office of Dancy's solicitor, Jacob Twisden, and are traced
back to Dancy himself who had used them to pay a " debt
of honour." Twisden himself shows by his conduct that

there is a sanction beyond *esprit de corps*, namely, integrity and justice. The presence of the Jew in gentile society, however unlovable he personally may be (and de Levis *is* unlovable), is indeed always a test of the quality of its justice.

De Levis is not a very comprehensive study in Jewish social psychology; he has no religious consciousness, either positive or negative. But in the play it is rather the social psychology of the English in their reaction to the Jew which is under scrutiny. De Levis illustrates well the dramatic situation of the Jew who is never quite accepted as a full member of the group and who reacts to the subtle discrimination by acute nervousness, suspicion, vindictiveness, and envy. His position has thus something in common with that of Shylock, and indeed many a passage in the play shows the influence of Shakespeare's study of the Jew in a hostile environment. But de Levis's final reaction when the climax is reached is quite different, and in a way more convincing, than Shylock's (convincing, that is, as realistic Jewish psychology). He turns up at the solicitor's office to make it clear that he has no interest in pressing the case to a conclusion now that he has been proved morally right:

> Don't mistake me. I didn't come because I feel Christian ; I am a Jew. I will take no money—not even that which was stolen. Give it to a charity. I'm proved right. And now I'm done with the damned thing.

De Levis has the vices of an industrious go-getter for whom material calculations matter more than they should; but he is, unlike Shylock, neither mean nor avaricious, and indeed he has that oriental love of colour and display, and those bursts of magnanimity and ostentation so lacking in Shylock but so characteristic of even very ordinary Jews. Galsworthy of course had the advantage (that Shakespeare lacked) of seeing Jews close up, and he used his opportunities to good purpose. Whilst not producing a work of classic depth or spiritual insight, he nevertheless produced a very interesting, and also very true, social document. The middle-class objection to Jews voiced by one of the characters, illustrates Galsworthy's power of irony and the keenness of his observation:

> They work harder ; they're more sober ; they're honest ; and they're everywhere. I've nothing against them, but the fact is—they get *on* so.

This scientific and judicial study of the Jewish problem as a social issue, shows us that the attempt is to be made to humanise the figure of the Jew in literature and to try to strip it of mythical features. And that is the dominant trend in the twentieth century. The Jew tends to be de-mythologized, to become neutral, to resemble any other middle class citizen. In the century of the common man the Jew has become the quintessential symbol of that common man!

This is evidently the tendency in the portrayal of Leopold Bloom in James Joyce's *Ulysses* (1922), probably the most important twentieth century work of fiction in which the Jew occupies the centre of interest. But Bloom is no longer " the Jew " of Dickens or of George Eliot; he is—at least on the surface—undistinguished and unheroic. He is simply unaccommodated man himself—Everyman in short—going about, through the space of one day and one night, his simple and everyday avocations.

The figure of Bloom had originally been suggested to Joyce by the story of a Dublin Jew named Hunter who was rumoured to be a cuckold. Additional features of Bloom's situation and character were provided by a friend and benefactor of Joyce, Ettore Schmitz (Svevo), an assimilated Jewish manufacturer of Trieste with some literary talent. Bloom does not have much association with Jews and Judaism, but there are authentic touches. Hebrew phrases go round in his head. There is a recurrent reference to an illustrated prospectus issued by an association of Palestine orange-growers (*Agudath Netaim*) which Bloom has been carrying round in his pocket throughout the day in his life which the novel records. Joyce also found in Bloom a reflection of his own problems. Having left his hometown of Dublin in 1904 after an unsettled youth and a Catholic upbringing, Joyce evidently found in the Jews an analogy to himself and his own situation. He too was an exile and a wanderer. But so was mankind as a whole. In this respect it may be said that we are all Jews!

Ulysses is the first major novel in which the Jew functions as a symbol of a universal condition. And that universal condition can be summed up in the word *alienation*. Victim, impotent lover, cuckold, dreamer, and frustrated wanderer, Bloom represents some of the permanent features of the twentieth century view of man: he resembles the anti-heroes of Kafka, Faulkner, and Bellow. In short he has become a *persona* of Everyman. We sense something abnormal in the man who claims to have a fixed and assured relation to his environment. Alienation has become the normal condition of mankind, and it is the great distinction of Joyce to have seen this so early on and to have given this phenomenon a classic literary expression in the figure of Bloom-Everyman.

Bloom is also a clown, and as such he arouses in the reader the traditional comic reaction associated with the Jew figure in earlier literature. And it is not only the Jew who is a clown. Twentieth century man has frequently seen himself in the image of a clown—helpless, absurd, and vainly trying to make sense of a hostile, or at least uncongenial, environment. In this respect Bloom is the precursor of Charlie Chaplin, Willy Loman, and of Vladimir and Estragon in Beckett's theatre of the absurd. At the end of the ' Cyclops ' episode in *Ulysses,* Bloom is seen being pursued out of Barney Kiernan's public house by the mordantly anti-semitic Citizen and his dog. Bloom escapes in a jarvey chased by the dog, whilst the Citizen hurls a biscuit-tin at his head which barely misses him. The scene is one of uproarious farce, pure clowning:

Did I kill him, says he, or what?
And he shouting to the bloody dog:
—After him Garry! After him, boy!
And the last we saw was the bloody car rounding the corner
and old sheepface on it gesticulating and the bloody mongrel
after it with his lugs back for all he was bloody well worth
to tear him limb from limb.

It is of course not true to say that *Ulysses* lacks the elements of the mythological. The whole scene of Bloom's exit from the pub is, as is well known, a parodic rendering of Ulysses' escape from the cave of the Cyclops in Homer's *Odyssey*. In Joyce's handling it becomes the escape of a very non-heroic Ulysses from a Dublin tavern with a roaring Citizen in pursuit temporarily ' blinded ' (like the Cyclops) because the sun is in his eyes. There is also mythological enlargement of another kind. With one of those Joycean lurches of tone which we encounter throughout the novel, Bloom becomes transformed momentarily into Elijah ascending to heaven in his chariot:

> When, lo, there came about them all a great brightness and they beheld the chariot wherein he stood ascend to heaven. And they beheld Him in the chariot, clothed upon in the glory of the brightness, having raiment as the sun, fair as the moon and terrible that for awe they durst not look upon him. And there came a voice out of heaven, calling: *Elijah! Elijah!* And he answered with a main cry: *Abba! Adonai!* And they beheld Him even Him, ben Bloom Elijah, amid clouds of angels ascend to the glory of the brightness at an angle of forty-five degrees over Donohue's in Little Green Street like a shot off a shovel.

Here notwithstanding the final note of bathos there is no doubt that the Jew Bloom has acquired a prophetic grandeur; the wonder of the past is upon him, " the glory of the brightness " looking absurdly out of place over Donohue's in Little Green Street.

Here once again is that conjunction of everyday beggary and sabbath magnificence with which Zangwill had endowned his characters, and ben Bloom Elijah as a comic rendering of the dual image is not entirely unlike that great king of schnorrers, Manasseh Bueno Barzilai Azavedo da Costa.

But Joyce's intuition of the dual image is subtler than this. And here we find a further myth-pattern. Throughout the length of the novel, Bloom is seeking his spiritual " son " Stephen Dedalus, whilst Stephen is seeking his spiritual " father " Bloom. Their union towards the end is all too short-lived, but it is in a way the climax of the story. Bloom finds in the young poet and intellectual a substitute for his own lost infant Rudy, whilst Stephen finds in the kind and unassertive middle-aged Jew a father-figure more congenial to him than his own natural father, the boorish Irishman Simon Dedalus. Bloom and Stephen thus fall into the classic pattern of unheroic father and attractive offspring that we find in *The Merchant of Venice*, *Ivanhoe*, and *Daniel Deronda* (Lapidoth and Mirah). Bloom is not black, not disreputable, but he has a tinge of grey: he is the *homme moyen sensuel*; whilst Stephen represents hope, beauty, and vision. Bloom's own line has come to an end; he has a daughter, but his son is dead, his wife unfaithful, and he himself impotent. But in the young Irishman with the Hellenic name who affirms the spirit of man in literature Bloom finds his true heir. It is a re-enactment of the Pauline fable of the olive-tree, with Stephen as the branch of the wild olive restored to the native root of the good olive tree. In the Homeric *schema* it is the reunion of Ulysses with his long-estranged son Telemechus—the home-coming of the wanderer, the intimation of a messianic fulfilment.

The Jewish mythic stereotypes which we have noted in earlier examples from lesser writers are thus still active, guiding both author and reader in their reaction to the rituals being enacted in the fable. For all the twentieth century desire to get behind the myth and depict the Jew on the basis of social realism, myth tends to return either unconsciously or in the form of burlesque. In George Bernard Shaw's play, *Man and Superman* the Jew-Devil figure of medieval legend returns in the burlesque form of Mendoza the Jewish bandit. Mendoza who meets the hero Tanner in the Sierra Nevada reappears later in his dream as the Devil, whilst Tanner himself is re-incarnated as Don Juan. The two proceed to an interesting discussion of love, metaphysics, and the future of the human race. But the real Devil-Jew still functions in the collective unconscious (as twentieth century anti-semitic propaganda has shown). In an actively religious sensibility such as that of Graham Greene he comes back to the surface.

Greene's *Brighton Rock* (1938) is a novel conducted at the level of theological symbolism or allegory. Pinkie is the villain, but he lives within the world of spiritual realities (*i.e.,* Catholic spirituality). He knows Heaven and Hell, Sin and Grace. On the other hand, the Jew, Colleoni, knows only the *World*. His self-possession is the sign of his utterly negative and corrupt function.

> His old Semitic face showed few emotions but a mild amusement, a mild friendliness ; but suddenly sitting there in the rich Victorian room, with the gold lighter in his pocket and the cigar case on his lap, he looked as a man might look who owned the whole world, the whole visible world that is, the cash registers and policemen and prostitutes, Parliament and the laws which say " this is Right and this is Wrong ".

Pinkie is damned : but Colleoni is not damned in the same way, for he is " the Prince of this World," *i.e.,* he is, in strictly theological terms, the Devil himself. Here is the old medieval conjunction of Jew and Devil. Colleoni subtly leads Pinkie on to his damnation and final catastrophe. He knows all that goes on in Pinkie's surroundings. His agents and his power are all pervasive. He does not personally commit acts of violence, but all the forces of evil are at his command.

Colleoni is not a Jew just by chance; he is rather *the* Jew. As he passes Pinkie in his car, he appears to symbolise the eternal Jew, " not Colleoni at all . . . but any rich middle-aged Jew returning to the Cosmopolitan after a concert in the Pavilion ". But if the Jew is the Devil, he is also (to complete the triangle) Judas. The attack on Spicer by " the Jews " (*i.e.*, Colleoni's gang) is a symbolic re-enactment of the crucifixion and betrayal of Jesus. Spicer's cry to Pinkie carries that particular theological reference when he exclaims in his anguish, " Pinkie. For Christ's sake."

A Gun For Sale (1936) presents the same Jew-Devil archetype in the person of Sir Marcus, ruler of the brothels and the steel industry. Through murder and conspiracy he manipulates the fate of nations and threatens the world with War. This will not only give a boost to the armaments industry (over which he presides) but will further his diabolical plans for the human race generally. In a transparently allegorical central scene, the heroine, Anne, and the main protagonist, Raven spend Christmas eve in a dark and freezing hut like the holy family, there being " no place for them at the inn." Like Christ, Raven will be killed through the forces of law and order, with the Jew in the background playing a sinister and dominant role. The fact that Raven is also a murderer gives an extra paradoxical twist but does not destroy the theological *schema*. On the contrary it serves to emphasize the fact that he bears upon himself the guilt of the human race, the burden of original sin which will be discharged at the moment of his passion. He gives up the ghost amid unbearable pain, and the world is saved, for the time being, from War.

This novel, like all Graham Greene's writings, combines the maximum of realism (sordid realism we should add) with the maximum of fantasy. In a way this gives a curious strength and tensile quality to his vision of everyday life whether in Brighton or Nottwich or the underside of London. But, nevertheless, realism is constantly subverted or side-tracked, and one finds oneself suddenly in a looking-glass world of medieval monsters and monks' tales. The authors of the medieval Mysteries dealt with the same range of myth and symbolism that Greene treats of, but they did not claim as he does to hold the mirror up to contemporary life. It is this double effort which gives to Graham Greene's work its tension and depth; but it also gives it a certain brittleness. It has a quality of prodigious anachronism. The portraits of Sir Marcus and Colleoni, with their medieval gargoyle features, are examples of such anachronism.

The fabulous Jew of Greene's imagination has counterparts in occasional parentheses in the work of T. S. Eliot—also, it should be noted, a poet strongly influenced by the Catholic tradition:

> My house is a decayed house,
> And the jew squats on the window sill, the owner,
> Spawned in some estaminet of Antwerp.

The word " spawned " serves to emphasise his subhuman nature. Elsewhere, however, Eliot is capable of voicing the medieval veneration of the *pre-Christian Jew* (*i.e.,* the prophets and heroes of the Old Testament):

> In the days of Nehemiah the Prophet ...
> In Shushan the palace, in the month Nisan,
> He served the wine to the king Ataterxes,
> And he grieved for the broken city, Jerusalem ;
> And the King gave him leave to depart
> That he might rebuild the city. ...
> So they built as men must build
> With the sword in one hand and the trowel in the other
> (Chorus from *The Rock,* 1934)

Here again determining the dividing line between the " good " Jew of Biblical times, and the " bad " Jew of to-day is the compulsive mechanism of the dual image.

The American Scene (*The Non-Jewish writers*)

In spite of the well-established myth of America as the melting-pot where races and nations would fuse together, and the stereotyped images of prejudice dividing one

national group from another would consequently disappear, the image of the Jew projected both in the work
of Jews and non-Jews on the North American continent
during the first half of the twentieth century does not differ
significantly from that which we have found in England.

Thomas Wolfe for a while enjoyed the favours of a
Jewish mistress who established him in the world of
wealthy and cultivated men of letters, yet in his writings
he vacillates between a fascination for the intensity and
vigour of Jewish life, and an almost obsessive disgust for
the persons of the New York Jews such as Mr. Rosen
(" Death and Proud Brother ") with his unctuousness, his
wealth, and his pearly teeth:

> He would wear striped trousers and he would walk up and
> down upon rich carpets, he would be splendid and full of
> power like a well-fed bull.

The medieval conjunction of Jew and Devil, still active
in the imagination of Graham Greene, has little theological
edge for the American writer sadly lacking as he is in a
sense of the middle ages, but something very like that
archetype is still discernible in F. Scott Fitzgerald's *The
Great Gatsby* (1925) in the portrait of Meyer Wolfsheim
" the man who fixed the World's Series back in 1919."
The reference is to the baseball championships of that
year, but the wording suggests manipulation on a universal
scale. This figure of ominous and diabolical power is a
" small flat-nosed Jew "; he has "bulbous fingers " and a
sentimental tendency to weep for friends who have met
a violent death.

Evil Jews are also to be found in the novels of Theodore
Dreiser. During the period of the rise of Nazism Dreiser
compromised himself as a spokesman of American anti-
semitism. He complained that the Jews were an obnoxious
racial entity.

> They do not blend as do other elements in this country,
> but retain, as they retain in all countries, their race solidarity
> and even their religion.

These words were written in 1935. Dreiser persisted almost until his death in 1945 in opposing to the standard liberal American attitude to Jews his own special right-wing prejudices—prejudices which have never really disappeared from the American consciousness although they may have been driven into that outer darkness where the Ku Klux Klan and the Birch Society still hold sway. And yet even Dreiser in *The Hand of the Potter* (1918) balances his evil characters with a fine old Jewish *pater familias* who is as noble as his son is evil—a reversal of the usual stereotyped juxtaposition of black father and white offspring. Dreiser's Jewish fathers are not all noble and patriarchal. In *The Titan* (1914) one of the hero Cowperwood's mistresses is the daughter of a certain Isadore Platow, a wealthy furrier of Chicago:

> He was a large, meaty, oily type of man—a kind of ambling, gelatinous formula of the male, with the usual sound commercial instincts of the Jew, but with an errant philosophy which led him to believe first one thing and then another so long as neither interfered definitely with his business.

Dreiser is pulling the stops a little too obviously. Such a description could almost have been written by a computer if it had been programmed with details of the standard Jewish " black " portraiture of the eighteenth and nineteenth centuries.

A somewhat more unusual anti-Semitic portrait which could certainly not have been manufactured by a computer is to be found in Ernest Hemingway's celebrated novel, *The Sun Also Rises* (1926). Robert Cohn is a Jew who in order to normalize his relationship with a hostile and cynical gentile world turns himself into a boxing champion. But in spite of his physical expertise and his success with the fascinating Lady Brett Ashley, he remains the outsider. He has successfully adapted himself to the *mores* of the tough set around him with their interest in the bull-fight (a typical Hemingway occupation), but the cloven hoof shows through in Cohn's unwillingness to get drunk like Jake, Bill, Mike, and other sound human specimens. The unhealthy sobriety of the Jew is as distasteful as his self-indulgence. Strangely enough, both are imputed to the Jew in the examples we are discussing, but then logical consistency is not a feature of myth. Hemingway is said to have drawn his character from the life, and if so it is easy to imagine that the real Robert Cohn was probably no more obnoxious than de Levis in Galsworthy's play. However, Hemingway has chosen to take the angle of vision of the hard bohemian characters who have trodden their moral sympathies underfoot. There is a Nietzschean transvaluation of values here, a refusal to admit the tenderer emotions, to temper toughness of mind, male aggressiveness, with any of the traditional Judeo-Christian virtues. Thus he kills those women characters who are too weak to share in the new dispensation (e.g., Catherine in *A Farewell to Arms*), he shuts out the undrinking Jew, and finally destroys himself as well. It is a plan ultimately destructive of human values.

The alien Jewish male is more often than not an un-attractive figure in earlier American fiction, but Leslie Fiedler has reminded us of the ubiquity of the desirable Jewish female, the archetypal " Jew's Daughter ". She appears in Hawthorne (*The Marble Faun*), in Melville (*Clarel*), and in a host of minor novelists. She may also be identified as Marjorie Morningstar, the good Jewess, beside the bad Jew, Noel Airman, in Herman Wouk's celebrated best-seller of 1955. There is a more serious portrait of the good Jew in Sinclair Lewis's *Arrowsmith* (1925). He is Professor Max Gottlieb, the true medical scientist, devoted, self-sacrificing, and holding aloft his ideals in a world of corruption and second-rate talent. The Jew as moral mentor appears in Richard Wright's classic negro novel *Native Son* (1940). Max is the Jewish lawyer who speaks to the heart of Bigger Thomas, the Negro convicted for murder and rape. The Jew being also an outsider and a victim may sympathize with the Negro and undersand his bitter and savage frustrations. Thus it is

Max, the Communist Jew, who discovers and saves the human image in the soul of the Negro. The novel reads a little sentimentally thirty years later when we are no longer so sure of finding a solution for all the world's racial problems in a socialist paradise. Moreover, we are no longer sure that for all their community of social experience the Negro and Jew are destined to walk hand in hand into a future of freedom and bliss. A latter-day Negro poet, LeRoi Jones gives us an image of the Jew the precise opposite of that projected in Wright's novel. He sees them as

> Selling fried potatoes
> and people, the little arty bastards
> talking arithmetic they sucked from the
> arab's head.

And he muses on——

> how we beat you
> and killed you
> and tied you up
> and marked this specimen
> "Dangerous Germ
> Culture." And put you back
> In a cold box.

Lurking behind the new sinister image of the Jew in Negro literature is the memory of the long hot summers of the sixties when Negro violence in a dozen cities made Jewish store-owners its chief victim, when the Negro proletariat saw in the successful Jewish bourgeoisie the symbol of all that it hated in America. Here in Richard Wright and in LeRoi Jones is an indication of the still potent contradictions set up by the archetypal dual image of the Jew.

Demythologizing the Jew

Is there any possibility of demythologizing the Jewish image? The fact is, as we have seen, that the Jew impinges on the non-Jew (and on himself) in a traumatic fashion. "The word *Jew*" Karl Shapiro has said, "retains its eternal shock." How is one to render this except by imputing either extraordinary virtue or extraordinary vice to the person who causes the shock? And that, of course is the way of mythology. The twentieth century has made a major effort to avoid this seeming necessity and to downtone the Jew, to neutralize him. We saw this process at work in the portrayal of Leopold Bloom in James Joyce's great novel, but we saw also that mythology returns in the mock-epic style and through the structure of relationships between the characters. Joyce's novel ultimately testifies to the permanence of the extraordinary in the portrayal of the Jew.

More decidedly neutral portraits of Jews appear in the novels of G. B. Stern, such as *Tents of Israel* (1924), and *The Young Matriarch* (1942). Except for their cosmopolitanism and the intensity of their family relationships and loyalties, they are like any other group of middle class folk. Plays on Old Testament subjects by Christopher Fry, Laurence Housman, and James Bridie also tend to treat the material in normal, tragic (or even sometimes, comic) terms. In much present-day American literature too the Jew becomes a neutral figure; he does not drag in the Jewish problem wherever he goes. This is true of the work of Pearl Buck, Damon Runyan and many others. But it may be suggested that the effort to neutralize the Jew has not really succeeded. A note of unreality creeps into the portraiture. The reader cannot convince himself that wings and/or cloven hoof are not somewhere hidden under the seemingly ordinary outer dress. Character-drawing is too disarming, too emphatically casual. No-one who is really like everyone else has to go out of his way to say so again and again.

This is ultimately the criticism that should be made against so distinguished a novel, for instance, as C. P. Snow's *The Conscience of the Rich* (1958). Snow has chosen to analyze the impact of the social and political changes of the '30's on a rich upper-class family of bankers, the Marches. The Marches are English Jews, but they have the instincts of the landed gentry. Jewish shading is provided by the rather strong sense of family loyalty, a feeling for the family's past generations, and a somewhat ritualized pattern of behaviour when they are together. But they are certainly not Jewish in any fundamental way.

> The Marches were secure, they were part of the country, *they lived almost exactly the lives of other wealthy men.* (my italics.)

The crisis comes when the son Charles decides to forego the family fortune and the responsibilities that go with it, marry a communist, and go in for a medical career. Charles though earnest, is not a moral visionary or an interpreter and critic of society like Stewart Ansell in E. M. Forster's novel. In Snow's novel, the detached spectator is a non-Jew, Lewis Eliot. It is he who observes the doings of the Marches and their upper class world from the position of middle class independence, whilst the Jew has become part of the fixed order of English life with little to distinguish him from his social background.

We have been suggesting that to neutralize the portrait of the Jew in this way, to make him ordinary and everyday, is to lean over backwards. The note of unreality creeps in through the very lack of polarization. To this it might be objected that there are, as a matter of fact, ordinary Jews who live lives scarcely distinguishable from those of non-Jews belonging to the same social class, and that C. P. Snow was almost undoubtedly painting the Marches from the life. He had observed just such a Jewish family. One cannot deny that Snow's novel and similar writings by G. B. Stern and others have *descriptive* truth and that the characterization often carries conviction. What is wrong is the plot, or more precisely, the *history* of the characters—the things that happen to them. The fact is that Jewish history is not neutral history. As George Eliot had sensed, the things that happen to Jews are not things that happen to ordinary people. Galsworthy also understood this. De Levis in *Loyalties* is an unextraordinary person, but his dramatic situation has the specificity of Jewish existence. This is what is lacking in *The Conscience of the Rich.* There is an existential gap. Jews living in the twentieth century cannot be isolated from Jewish history without some prejudice to the realism of the portraiture. Jewish history may not be enjoyable for those living it, but friend and foe will surely agree that it is nothing if not remarkable.

It may be suggested that the only satisfactory way of demythologizing the Jew is to take the emphasis off the Jew as a person and to place it on Jewish history. It is first and foremost Jewish history which makes the Jew strange and remarkable, not the supposed extremes of his personality. This is the implication of a work by an American non-Jewish writer which should be mentioned. It is John Hersey's *The Wall* (1950), the story of the Warsaw Ghetto revolt and the Jewish martyrdom at the hands of the Nazis—a theme central to modern Jewish history and of immense importance for the literary portrayal of the Jew from now onwards. *The Wall* presents its Jewish characters in the Ghetto as—in the first instance—perfectly ordinary everyday characters; some of them are noble, some ignoble; but most of them have ordinary human failings and weaknesses. This we may say, so far, is the neutral or journalistic portrayal of the Jew—and Hersey is first of all a journalist. But we become quickly aware that the extraordinary *history* in which these people are involved—and indeed have always been involved—creates of them in the end fabulous personalities. The elements of heroism, nobility, and an inner sense of superiority in the face of evil, seem to be bestowed upon the Jew by the very nature of his situation. It is this which Hersey recognizes as the final meaning of the Ghetto tragedy. Jewish history is not neutral history; it is the history of trial and sacrifice. The Jew becomes inevitably a symbol of the moral victory of the human spirit, not because as an individual he is necessarily better than anyone else, but evidently because he is called upon to be a witness to the work of God in the world. The " Suffering Servant " acquires a dignity not on account of his character but on account of his situation. It is an existential not a moral distinction which primarily marks the Jew out from his fellows. And in this Hersey has come near to a valid rendering of the Jewish image for the twentieth century reader.

In a poetically conceived novel from the Antipodes, *Riders in the Chariot* (1961), Patrick White records the spiritual impact of the Holocaust on one Himmelfarb, a German Jewish professor who has survived Auschwitz to settle down as a labourer in a small Australian township. As well as being a "suffering servant," he is also a visionary, a mystic. But his vision of the "Chariot," though serving to define his specific Jewish existence, also links him mysteriously with other suffering characters—an eccentric maiden lady who finds the Chariot in trees and animals, and a half-educated Negro artist who has achieved it in paint.

The Jewish fate is what makes the Jew different, but it can be shared by others whose lives have been touched by the same magic spell of triumph and tragedy.

CHAPTER FIVE

JEWISH WRITERS IN SEARCH OF IDENTITY

Jewish writers in the twentieth century have shown a remarkable degree of articulateness. In England, though few have attained first rank, their contribution to the shaping of the Jewish image through reflection and description has been of considerable importance. An early example of Jewish portraiture which achieved a high degree of pathos was I. Goller's *The Five Books of Mr. Moses* (1929). The inspiration of Zangwill's Ghetto tales was felt in the work of Louis Golding, whose *Magnolia Street* (1932) seemed at one moment to be establishing itself as a minor classic. On closer scrutiny, however, it is revealed as a sentimental version of the Jewish problem; it lacks the seriousness, the depth, the vivid and strikingly Jewish humour of Zangwill's classical work. From the two sides of Magnolia Street, Jew and gentile face one another. Normally they are apart, divided by prejudice and social distinctions, but the great moments of the book come when the barriers are down. Benny Edelman rescues Tommy Wright from drowning and becomes the hero of the day for both sides of Magnolia Street; or the romance of John Cooper and Rose Berman, culminating in their inter-marriage, serves to inter-weave the two communities in a rather lush sentimental glow of nuptial concord. Zangwill was aware of the historical forces making for separatism, and of the precariousness, indeed the mortal peril, of abandoning it (though his characters do often abandon it); with Golding it is as easy as crossing the street.

That is what is meant by saying that his is fundamentally a sentimental portrait of the Jew in a Christian society. Rose Berman's philosophy seems to be that of Golding:

> As if it mattered about people being Jews and not being Jews, as if the heart wasn't just the same heart, and being born or marrying or dying was Jewish or not Jewish.

In *Mr. Emmanuel, Golding's* reaction to the Hitler episode reveals the same inadequacy. Hitler was to show that it did matter very much about people being Jews and not being Jews. But Golding's hero, being a saintly humanitarian and a liberal, does not quite understand the real historical forces at work. He finds himself in Berlin and eventually in a concentration camp—but all the time he is really blinking rather childishly at the strange facts that confront him: an out-of-date nineteenth century liberal lost amid the jungle of twentieth century hatreds and fears. Indeed, the sentimental version of the Jewish problem, for which the appropriate solution is seen in inter-marriage and a pleasant association of all people of goodwill on both sides of the street, does not begin to touch the harsh realities of the problem as they affect a serious writer aware of the urgent realities of modern history. Neither the anguish of Jewish existence nor the self-betraying efforts to escape from it, have any meaning for the sentimentalist. He is merely concerned to make interesting and entertaining stories filled with Jewish local colour and a flavouring of out-of-date philosophy.

The Jews who react seriously to the problems of Jewish existence may do so either in a positive or negative way: if the latter, we find something of that Jewish self-repulsion so noticeable in Simone Weil and Marcel Proust. Proust's treatment of the Jewish problem, incidentally, is more complex than is usually recognised. In the death of Swann, something of the sombre pride and fortitude of Jewish heroism is indicated; but normally the Jewish side of Proust's sensibility reveals itself as marked by self-hatred streaked through with excessive self-possession. Up to about the middle of this century it was unusual for a Jewish writer to treat the Jewish question, *i.e.* the question of Jewish identity, with indifference. He might be for or against, but to treat the matter sentimentally (like L. Golding) or neutrally (like G. B. Stern) was rare, and could without injustice be castigated as a sign of spiritual inadequacy.

However, a number of important writers of Jewish origin and background have shown in the last twenty years or so that it is possible to use Jewish subject matter and characters whilst ignoring the problem of Jewish identity. There has been a dramatic increase in Jewish folklore and the use of Yiddish expressions but a corresponding decrease in religious and existential depth. Perhaps there is an unconscious feeling that the " Jewish Problem " as such, i.e. the problem of Jewish existence and its purpose, has been taken over by the State of Israel, leaving the Jewish writer in the Diaspora free to devote himself to " wider " themes, to the human condition in general. At the same time the new found Jewish national self-respect legitimates the use of Jewish local colour on an extensive scale. Some such unconscious changing of the guard would explain the fact that this new trend—very much more marked as we shall see in the United States—has coincided chronologically with the establishment of the State of Israel.

Wolf Mankowitz's brief novels of East End life (such as *A Kid for Two Farthings* and *Make Me an Offer*) present Jewish characters whose Judaism is almost completely muted. A bespoke tailor, a dealer in antiques, an amateur boxer—such characters have plenty of human interest but very little, except an occasional phrase or gesture or a touch of gentle old-world sadness, to indicate their Jewishness. Mr. Mankowitz's skill as a short story writer is considerable and his dialogue has a quite distinctive wry humour. It may also be said that he has a feeling for symbolism (the unicorn in *A Kid for Two Farthings* has a genuine symbolic function) and a touch of pathos, both of a distinctly Jewish kind, but he would no doubt be the first to admit that the Jewish problem as such and the problem of the Jew and his neighbour were not at this time the most compelling problems in his world. Mankowitz has since undergone a certain spiritual awakening as a result of the War of 1967 and its revelation of Israel's power of self-renewal. He declared himself galvanized by the events of that summer. When the *shofar* was sounded at the Western Wall of the Temple he said, " The stone heart of Jewish memory broke and returned to life." This we may suspect will have its effect on his writing.

Bernard Kops has a strong feeling for Jewish life and values, but they tend to be symbols of a wider human predicament (*The Hamlet of Stepney Green*, 1956). This is also true of *Yes From No-man's Land* (1965), a novel told through the stream of consciousness of a dying Jew in whose mind the memory of the Holocaust, of Eastern Europe, of poverty and struggle in the East End of London during the thirties, combine with meditations on life in Israel to form an authentic landscape of historic Jewish experience. Joe Levene is discovering and affirming his Jewish identity on his death-bed in the Hackney Hospital. " The Jews," he affirms, " are the heart of the world." But it is an ironic perspective. He is dying, his family is breaking up; his son Barry will neither carry on the traditions, nor will he even beget children to continue the life of the old man; and Joe will be gently eased out of this world by the kindly nuns who are nursing him, and for whom his Jewish reminiscences and resentments are merely the delirium of a poor dying soul. The work has considerable power, but it is ultimately an elegy for the passing of the Jew and his faith.

The same East London background is shared by two other distinguished dramatists of the mid-century, Arnold Wesker and Harold Pinter. Jewish characters appear fairly often in both writers, but it can hardly be said that they have any specific concern with the inner tensions of Jewish society (either by way of affirmation or of revolt). The final play of the "Wesker Trilogy" is entitled "I'm Talking About Jerusalem" (1960). The principal characters are Jewish, but the wandering Jews function merely as a catalyst for a general feeling of frustration associated with the mood of the post-war generation. Dave Simmonds's search for vision, the vision of Jerusalem, symbolizes mankind's undefeated hope for the future. It has no special Jewish properties. Naturally, world salvation is and has always been a Jewish theme, and Jerusalem as locality and ideal is its authentic symbol. But balancing this universalism there was always a sense of a particular people having a particular task, and particular obsessions which marked them out from their environment. What is missing in the writers of the mid-century is the question that Kipling's child-hero asks himself, "Who is Kim?". It is the question of fundamental identity. In the absence of such a question, the appearance of Jewish characters, even if they are the central characters in a novel or play, tends to be merely accidental.

Other writers since the Second World War have remained more within the psychic zone of Jewish history. Mr. Mordecai Richler introduces Jews in a rather casual way in his post-war novel *The Acrobats* (1954), but he does manage to indicate, briefly but incisively, something of the anguish of the Jew's existence, the crisis of his identity, and to locate the inner conflicts of the Jew in their context of modern suffering and universal conflict. In this book, he collects examples of the human flotsam left over by the Second World War: there are assorted Communists, an ex-Nazi camp guard, perverts, artists, and two Jews. The Jewish problem is not central, but in the novel's attempt to discover some sort of faith still possible for men, the Jew, Chaim, is felt to have the nearest thing to a solution. He still preserves something of love, loyalty, and tolerance—virtues picked out by accurate, though somewhat incongruous, quotations from Maimonides and the Rabbis of the Talmud. Over against him, by contrast, is the bad Jew, Barney. Barney is an American *bourgeois* married to an idle self-seeking Jewess, and betraying something of that Jewish self-contempt and that materialism typical of his kind. Chaim's ambition is to go to Israel to find a new life there based on Jewish self-respect (though it is typical of the mood of futility in which the book is conceived that he ends up in Paris, not Jerusalem). Barney hates the cossacks but his ambition is to dine with their generals! Here is the dual image which the Jew projects in post-war society.

In *The Apprenticeship of Duddy Kravitz* (1959), Richler interiorizes these contradictions in a single character. His protagonist, Duddy is the land-hungry, unscrupulous young go-getter from the Jewish ghetto of Montreal. In his struggle for material possessions and success he leaves behind him broken lives and bodies. He despises the *goyim*, yet he remains loyal to his family and obsessively proud of his race. It is he more than anyone who holds the family together in a disintegrating universe. And to this his uncle Benjy testifies on his deathbed. "I'd look at you and see a busy, conniving little yid, and I was wrong because there was more, much more."

The Bankrupts (1958) by Brian Glanville inaugurated a " New Wave " of Anglo-Jewish novels the general inspiration for which may be traced to the writings of the " angry young men " of the fifties led by John Osborne whose play " Look Back in Anger " (1956) began the trend. Glanville and several other writers who followed him, such as Dan Jacobson and Frederic Raphael, translated this trend into Jewish terms. They are looking back in anger at Anglo-Jewish family life and its social pattern. The stance is not particularly new. We find it at the end of the nineteenth century in Zangwill's *Children of the Ghetto* and in Amy Levy's *Reuben Sachs*—the latter a quite bitter attack on the materialism of the rising Jewish middle class of the period. But in Glanville's novel the Jewish middle class is felt to have sunk more fatally into

materialism and hardness of heart, and the author's criticism is consequently more mordant and uncompromising.

A new element is also provided in the form of a radical
revolt against the sexual *mores* (or supposed sexual *mores*)
of the older generation. Here we may detect some confusion with the notorious prudery and restrictiveness of
the middle-class Puritan tradition in England. Victorian-
ism is not exactly a Jewish disease. Jews have generally
shown a positive attitude to family, and a refreshing
honesty regarding sexual relations. Restrictions there have
always been—they are part of the Biblical code—but
Judaism is really guiltless of the duplicities and hypocrisies
which marked the Victorian world of Dickens, Thackeray,
and Ibsen. As for the ban on inter-marriage, that has
been directed rather by considerations of group loyalty
than by sexual squeamishness. In all, there is some distortion here of the type that we have observed frequently
in non-Jewish authors. The Jewish God becomes guilty
of the sins of the spirit from which western society has
suffered in the post-Victorian era.

There is novelty also in the emphasis on a sociological
revolt against middle-class standards with which the Jew
(following the teachings of Max Weber) is identified.
Admirers of the middle class and of Jews had made the
same identification. In Scott and in E. M. Forster, as we
saw earlier, the Jews stood as the protagonists of the sturdy
bourgeois virtues of trade and honesty against the decayed
values of the chivalry. Now in the twentieth century the
middle classes are under fire and the Jew has become a
principal target. The proletarian ideal of D. H. Lawrence
and others is joined to the law of instinct, whilst middle-
class (Jewish) respectability is seen as the enemy of the
passionate life of nature and freedom.

The truth of the matter is that the whole twentieth
century social revolution involving the assertion of the
working-class world and its values against the emptiness
of bourgeois liberalism has little relevance to the Jewish
scene. Or if anything the Jews are on both sides of the

barricades. We should not forget, as Leopold Bloom would have said, that Marx and Trotsky were Jews. Nor should middle-class supporters forget that the Jews have a long aristocratic tradition as well. Disraeli claimed they were the natural aristocrats of mankind. Certainly romance and adventure are in their blood just as much as the domestic virtues and the instinct of trade. Byron knew this; Scott evidently did not.

Before we leave the novelists, mention may be made of a remarkable Jewish novel which does not belong to any established type or category. It is Adele Wiseman's *The Sacrifice* (1956). This moving book by a Canadian Jewess is, at one level, a story of modern Jewish life on the American continent retailed with the realism of a Faulkner or a Hemingway; at another level, it is a translation into modern terms of the story of the Patriarchs, and as such is reminiscent of the Miracle plays of the middle ages or of Thomas Mann's Biblical novels in our own century. Its genuine seriousness and tragic depth are a pleasing departure from the tradition of the modern Anglo-Jewish novel.

The three principal characters are Abraham, Sarah and their son Isaac. Isaac eventually marries Ruth, whose relationship with the family likewise falls into the pattern of her Biblical prototype, the semi-alien who is destined to bear the seed of promise. The chief character, Abraham, is the man of spiritual intensities who tries to envision and shape the future in accordance with his high sense of a divine election governing the destinies of his People in general, and his own family in particular: " But as the villainies of the few may stand out, so will our faith, our grand desire. It is for this we are chosen." His fierce and high ambitions, his religious tenacity, are seen to result in the sacrifice of his son Isaac. In the agonising quarrel with his daughter-in-law which follows the death of his son, Abraham is rebuked: " You and God together are always thinking. Whatever is convenient for you, God happens to think. Where do you keep him, this God of yours, in your coat pocket? " Abraham remains the hero of the book throughout, but the attitude generated towards him has a certain ambiguity. He is both a patriarchal figure of nobility and courage — the man of trials and sufferings whose spirit has been humbled through the loss of his two older sons in a Polish pogrom—and also the man of pride whose spiritual earnestness is represented as not without its streak of egoism. His attempt to control the lives of his children is seen to lead to disaster. He ends his life in insanity and disgrace, his world having crashed about him in ruins. This version of the dual image is evidently more subtly interiorized than that of Richler or Glanville. It issues from a more anguished centre of personal crisis.

Among the Anglo-Jewish poets of the twentieth century, we are struck first by the contribution of Isaac Rosenberg, a First-War poet of considerable lyric power. Although he is concerned with the general human tragedy of the War, with " the pity war distilled," he displays both in his war poetry and his earlier work a considerable interest in the Jew as an image of lonely strife. The interrogative form of these poems is suggestive. Behind them is the question of Jewish identity, of why the Jew is marked out for peculiar trials and tribulations:

> Moses, from whose loins I sprung,
> Lit by a lamp in his blood
> Ten immutable rules, a moon
> For mutable lampless men.

> The blonde, the bronze, the ruddy,
> With the same heaving blood,
> Keep tide to the moon of Moses,
> Then why do they sneer at me?
> ("The Jew")

Rosenberg died young, and when he died his Jewish self-consciousness had not yet been fully awakened. He was sufficiently attracted by the story of Moses to write a verse drama on it, and also by the theme of the legendary

Lilith, though he hardly achieved that " fruitful fusion between English and Hebrew culture " which Siegfried Sassoon attributed to him. But there is a certain moral and religious emphasis in his best poems about the Great War which is recognizably Jewish. His sense of loneliness and personal inadequacy, so marked both in his poems and letters, sometimes issues in that cry to God which takes us back to *Job* and to the tragic poets of the exile.

> My Maker shunneth me.
> Even as a wretch stricken with leprosy
> So hold I pestilent supremacy.
> Yea! He hath fled as far as the uttermost star,
> Beyond the unperturbed fastnesses of night,
> And dreams that bastioned are
> By fretted towers of sleep that scare His light.
>
> (" Spiritual Isolation ")

Had Rosenberg lived longer we may well suppose that he would have thought more about his Jewish origins and that this would have resulted in work of greater Hebraic richness. One critic has detected in him the beginning of a genius similar to that of Blake who modelled himself so much on the prophets of the Hebrew Bible. Rosenberg is like Blake in many ways, not least in an erotic strain of poetry laced with imagery of Eden and the *Song of Songs*. But Blake's ambivalent attitude to the Hebrew tradition should not be forgotten. The Bible provided him with a source of sensual imagery and delight—the poetry of the Bible was the only true poetry—but it was also to be condemned for its harsh system of moral restrictions. Rosenberg, sharing something of the same mood, voices his opposition to the " ancient God " of the Old Testament and his moral law. ("The Female God," 1914). The Bible legislates for earthly man, for his senses, but it does *legislate*—it controls, it limits, and therefore it is the enemy of the free imagination and of free sexuality. It is in this form that the dual image operates for many poets of the romantic tradition whose feelings for the Biblical God is marked by alternate (or simultaneous) moods of attraction and repulsion:

> Your wealth
> Is but his cunning to make death more hard,
> Your iron sinews take more pain in breaking;
> And he has made the market for your beauty
> Too poor to buy, although you die to sell.
>
> ("God")

Mr. Emanuel Litvinoff, a poet of the Second World War, shows a somewhat healthier adjustment to his Jewish heritage. This is partly due to the memory of the Holocaust which has seared itself into the consciousness of all. The non-Jew is now called to judgment. The Jew may bear his insult with pride (like the King of Denmark when offering to put on the yellow badge). The Jew for his part is not called upon to vindicate himself against his vilifiers. Thus Litvinoff addresses an angry but dignified rebuke to an older fellow-poet, T. S. Eliot:

> I am not one accepted in your parish.
> Bleistein is my relative, and I share
> the protozoic slime of Shylock, a page
> in Stürmer, and underneath the cities,
> a billet somewhat lower than the rats.
> Blood in the sewers. Pieces of our flesh
> float in the ordure on the Vistula.
> You had a sermon but it was not this ...
>
> Yet walking with Cohen when the sun exploded
> and darkness choked our nostrils,
> and the smoke drifting over Treblinka
> reeked of the smouldering ashes of children,
> I thought what an angry poem
> You would have made of it, given the pity.

The dark image of the Jew projected in several poems of T. S. Eliot is something that the Jew need no longer apologize for: it is an obscenity which Eliot himself has to explain. As far as the Jew is concerned, the very gesture of apology or evasion becomes a betrayal of the six million martyrs. Litvinoff walks with Cohen when the sun exploded. It is a place of honour.

A similarly positive adjustment to the indignities of
Jewish history is achieved in the work of one of the most
serious of the younger generation of Anglo-Jewish poets
of the sixties, Mr. Nathaniel Tarn. In his kabbalistically
inspired poems he combines images of Auschwitz with
messianic fantasies, the sign above the gas-chamber repre-
senting the entrance into the Kingdom of Heaven en-
visioned by the founder of Hassidism:

> The North has turned black: black for putrefied blood.
> The convoys smoke towards it, the cattle trucks groan.
> I see the bone and skin shops they'll open with our meat.
> Here are the baths, the paradise fountains.
> The doors will say with big placards 'Enter and be cleansed'.
> Children will play with their elder's fringes.
> Stifling in the funny gas they will praise the Name I sell them.
> This is the world to come, this and no other.
> You are flushed into the Kingdom with gay gas sneezes.
>
> (" The Master of the Name in his Privy ")

In a dialectical fashion he sees the murder of the six
million as the preliminary to a world-saving event. In
the world after the flood, the gardens on Ararat are
manured with Jewish remains:

> This is a Jewish century you lot,
> this compost is of falcon noses and shark lips.
>
> (" Noah on Ararat Again ")

Again the mocking scorn at the *Stürmer* image of the
Jew. With deluge comes salvation. Noah is at work again
represented in the absurd resilience of Jewish existence
after the Holocaust:

> The Lord builds His pulse into the creeping things of the deep,
> climbs into trees with them and settles on earth ;
> His stroke guides birds in the air, homes them to Ararat,
> at right angles to the sun.

In a meditation on the famous Strasbourg image of the
defeated synagogue as a blindfolded woman with a broken

staff, Tarn ponders the paradoxes of the broken house of Israel, doomed, as the medieval Christian church supposed, to spiritual extinction. Again the imagery of the extermination camp:

> The worm has made his way through books how they
> crumble
>
> fire his through the parchment of scholars' hides
> the house of study their benches tables lights
> are no longer as much as smoke in the sky or a crow's
> feather
> they have rubbed out our names from the library of the holy
> word
> (From " The Beautiful Contradictions," 1969)

—but he ends with a wedding, the wedding of the shattered and ragged house of Israel with the female image of the deserted synagogue:

> I shall have time to spare beside you. I shall have time to spare
> You shall have sons my love   unnumbered as the ghosts.

The hope for the future is whimsical and absurd, but not the less tenacious for being born out of the heart of despair.

CHAPTER SIX

THE AMERICAN JEWISH RENAISSANCE

The Earlier Phrase

There is little in American Jewish writing prior to the
Second World War to prepare us for the extraordinary
flowering of talent which has since then placed the Jews,
especially of New York, in a position of literary supremacy
unknown before in the history of the Diaspora. Earlier
writers such as Abraham Cahan, Ludwig Lewisohn, or
even Henry Roth and Daniel Fuchs did not enjoy the
kind of attention now given to Bernard Malamud, Philip
Roth and Saul Bellow. Those earlier writers had a more
limited, parochial theme, and though this was their
strength, it also limited their audience. They reflected the
problem of dual living through the prism of consciousness
of the Jewish immigrant of the first or second generation.
It is the same theme as that of Israel Zangwill, and indeed
Zangwill's *Children of the Ghetto,* first published in the
United States, may stand as the prototype of this kind of
fiction, a fiction which concerns itself primarily with the
search for identity which goes on in the soul of the Jew,
man or child, who perforce lives in two worlds. Zangwill's
English localities may be simply translated into American
equivalents: for the East End, read the lower east side of
Manhattan, and for Golder's Green, read Washington
Heights. Later on Zangwill contributed once more to
American Jewish letters in a sentimental play, *The Melting
Pot* (1908) on the theme of American Jewry and its dream
of total assimilation.

Cahan's novel *The Rise of David Levinsky* (1917)

presents the classic theme of the Jewish immigrant who brings his burden of Jewish spirituality into an alien environment to which he rapidly and successfully adapts himself. From this new world of *laissez-faire* brutality the Jewish God is conspicuously absent. Neither the Jewish sabbath nor the Jewish social ethic which had made life bearable in the east European ghetto has any place there. But like the characters of Zangwill, David Levinsky does not abandon his inner Jewish heritage of values— indeed he cannot for they are too much a part of himself —and looking back from his position of material success he testifies to this fact:

> When I take a look at my inner identity it impresses me as being precisely the same as it was thirty or forty years ago.

This is only a half-truth, for the fact is that his Jewish identity has been interiorized: it is a candle within doors. Inwardly he still cherishes the holy light of the Talmud Torah school in Antomir where he was brought up in poverty, whilst in his social and even his sexual relations he is like Cowperwood, the protagonist of Dreiser's great trilogy—a successful, and unscrupulous commercial magnate. But he is conscious of the price he has paid for El Dorado, and its glitter turns to dust as he surveys the richer treasures which he had left behind. In this he is like the hero of Zangwill's brief tale, *Diary of a Meshummad*.

A closer and more poignant analysis of this kind of alienation is provided in Henry Roth's *Call It Sleep* (1934). This, like Cahan's novel, is a semi-autobiographical account by a first generation immigrant, but it is more precisely focused, confining its purview to the experiences of a child living on the edge of the Jewish ghetto on the lower east side of New York. David Schearl, lost, bewildered and friendless, is a victim from the start. His oedipal home background is symbolic of the life of the new immigrant child; there is a stern and punishing father, and a loving mother whose Yiddish speech and warm physical embrace are all that protect the child from an alien world. In a larger sense the duality of the child's life is mapped out by his relationship with his English-speaking companions of the one side, and by his family setting on the other, with its different standards, its rituals, and its higher tone of speech. Walter Allen locates the duality of the lives of Roth's characters with reference to this double-standard of speech. He notes that the yiddish speech of the Schearls is rendered for the purpose of the novel in a remarkably pure English, that of cultivated folk, whilst in conversation with the other slum dwellers—Italian, Irish, Hungarian, etc. they speak an almost incomprehensible distortion of the English language. Here is the semantic aspect of the dual image, and Walter Allen perceptively concludes that " there is a sense in which the Schearls are in the slums but not of them." They are living their own different lives inwardly.

But the graces of a better way of life are not only preserved in the yiddish speech of the home and in the loving embrace of David's mother: the novel has a religious dimension as well. Reb Yidel Pankower is a caricature of the well-known type of harsh Talmud Torah teacher. He belongs with David's father to the world of punishment, of inhuman and incomprehensible terrors. It is his father who sends him to the Rabbi's cheder to be made a Jew of, and there he suffers from the cheder teacher's ill-temper and occasional outbursts of violence for which the child's tender and imaginative sensibilities are entirely unadapted. It is a classic situation made familiar to us in the writings of Peretz and Bialik. But the rabbi is not of one piece. His personality also harbours ambiguities, for behind the rabbi's voice David also hears the echo of the great words of Isaiah that are being taught to the top class; and the words express a glory and a terror which transcend the drab universe which David inhabits:

' In the year that King Uzziah died, Isaiah saw God. And God was sitting high on his throne, high in heaven and in his temple. . . . But when Isaiah saw the Almighty in His majesty and His terrible light—Woe me! he cried, What

shall I do! I am lost.' The Rabbi seized his skull-cap and
crumpled it. ' I, common man, have seen the Almighty, I,
unclean one have seen him! Behold my lips are unclean
and I live in a land unclean. . . .'

The application not only to the Rabbi but to David and
his whole generation is clear. For David the text becomes
the key to his final epiphany when, double-dared by his
companions, he is nearly electrocuted through placing a
zinc bar between the car-tracks on Tenth Street. It is then
that he sees the great light of Isaiah's vision flashing up
to consume him. Through the terror of that moment
David passes from childhood to maturity, and the oedipal
crisis is, symbolically at least, overcome. His initiation
is over, but burned though he is with holy fire, he will
still remain an outsider in an unclean land.

The poets, Hyam Plutzig, Delmore Schwartz, and Karl
Shapiro have likewise given sharp symbolic expression
to the existential duality of the American Jew. In one
poem Plutzig portrays a typically successful Jewish middle
class citizen standing well-dressed beside his shining auto-
mobile, but haunted by a history measured (unlike that
of North America) in thousands of years. Looking at him
a little more closely the poet notes " the shirt of Nessus "
on his skin. We remember that it is through the shirt of
the Centaur that the past takes its revenge on Hercules:
it signifies at once the treachery of Hercules and the retribution which overtakes him.

Karl Shapiro in his *Poems of a Jew* ranges widely over
the past and present. He is particularly conscious of the
uniqueness of Jewish history symbolized by the letters of
the Hebrew alphabet (" The Alphabet "). They go back
twisting and tightening into the darkness of the past to
the beginning of time, and they also point to a future
consummation:

> These are the letters that all men refuse
> And will refuse until the king arrives
> And will refuse until the death of time
> And all is rolled back in the book of days.

Irving Malin is right in defining Shapiro as a poet of the exile. In "My Grandmother" he sees an aged Jewish lady, pious and dignified, a stranger in a strange land, "her dry and corded throat harangued by grief." She is a figure of exile:

> Taking her exile for granted, confusing
> The tongues and tasks of her children's children.

But with Shapiro the specific exile of the Jew is already blending into the universal experience of exile which is the fate of modern man. In his Preface he declares that since the hideous blood purge of the Jews by Germany, the Jew can no longer be viewed as either extraordinarily noble or extraordinarily despicable " but as man essentially himself, beyond nationality, defenseless against the crushing impersonality of history."

The New Jewish Writers

What do we mean by " the Jewish problem "? There are, it would seem, three distinct meanings as far as our subject is concerned. The first is the problem of the non-Jew in dealing with that foreign body known as the Jew. That is what Dreiser meant by saying that there was a Jewish problem in America, and that is also what Hitler meant when he spoke of the Jewish problem in Germany. The second meaning is the problem of Jewish identity as it presents itself in the reflex of Jewish self-awareness and in his social consciousness, as in Henry Roth and Abraham Cahan. It is the problem of the Jew in relation to his history and his environment. Various solutions have been attempted for this particular problem; one is assimilation, the other is Jewish national self-determination in Israel or elsewhere. In the third version of the Jewish problem, the whole accent is taken off the word 'Jewish', and the problematic nature of Jewish existence—the sense of alienation which the Jew experiences—becomes a symbol for mankind's alienation, for the general human quest for identity, for authentic life within and without.

The extraordinary centrality of Jews and Jewish themes in present-day American literature may be attributed chiefly to this universalization of the Jewish sense of alienation. At one time the experience of exile, of being a victim, lonely, harassed, burdened with a guilt not his own, served to separate the Jew from his fellow man. It was a Jewish predicament. Now such consciousness has become the common heritage of a whole generation of survivors and 'displaced persons.' We are all displaced. Auschwitz has entered deeply into the soul of modern man: it functions as a new fundamental metaphor, a new archetype. All mankind is waiting for Godot in a treeless wilderness in which fear, insult, and outrage form the quotidian reality. In these circumstances the Jew has become a paradigm for a universal reality.

This situation is illuminated in Delmore Schwartz's poem, "Abraham," He is speaking of Abraham's call to leave his father's house, and of the sacrifice of Isaac. In all this Abraham is not merely the father of the Jewish people, but clearly a " father of many nations "—an ancestor of alienated humanity at large:

> It has never been otherwise:
> Exiled wandering, dumbfounded by riches,
> Estranged among strangers, dismayed by the infinite sky,
> An alien to myself until at last the caste of the last alienation
> The angel of death comes to make the alienated and
> indestructible one a part of his famous and democratic society.

The sense of alienation provides the groundwork of the present revival of Jewish consciousness in literature: it provides the key in particular to the work of Saul Bellow, Bernard Malamud and Philip Roth. Roth's short story ' Eli the Fanatic ' may stand as a prototype of this trend. But it can be sensed in many other Jewish writers too. Arthur Miller even when he is not dealing directly with Jewish themes prominently features the ' post-Auschwitz ' mentality in such a play for instance, as " After the Fall." In " Incident at Vichy " (1964) the explicit theme is the universality of anti-semitism. Everyone, Jews included, requires a victim, a ' Jew '. That victim becomes the touchstone of a society's ethical standards. In that sense "Incident at Vichy " is not a Jewish play, nor is it a play about the " Jewish problem " in the classical sense. Paradoxically it announces the end of the Jewish problem. A more generalized landscape of suffering and victimization has taken its place.

Arthur Miller's presentation did not lack the elements of sentimental shading and rhetoric. But this cannot be said of Bernard Malamud's great novel *The Fixer* (1966). Here is a fastidiously conceived work, restrained, realistic, and yet powerful in its moral impact. Malamud, too, places the Jewish victim figure in a framework of universal concerns, but nothing is lost of the particularity of the portrait of Yakov Bok, a Russian Jew of the early twentieth century. The book is based on an infamous blood libel in consequence of which a certain Menahem Mendel Beilis, was charged with the ritual murder of a Russian boy in Kiev in 1911. Malamud has carefully sifted the historical materials and has certainly succeeded in penetrating the world of the Jews of the Russian pale and their mental habits. From this point of view the novel is something of a *tour de force* (like *The Natural* on the theme of American baseball). Yet ultimately it is an allegorical work: its theme is not Jewish suffering as such, its aetiology and purposed ends, but the experience of victimization in general. Yakov is, in Karl Shapiro's words, " man essentially himself, beyond nationality." The Investigating Magistrate, Bibikov, who comes to visit Yakov Bok in prison stresses this fact. If Yakov is in prison it is because Russia is one big prison in the year 1911 :

> In one sense we are all prisoners here . . . Keep in mind
> Yakov Shepsovitch, that if your life is without value, so
> is mine. If the law does not protect you, it will not, in the
> end, protect me. Therefore I dare not fail you. . . .

Bibikov who sympathizes with Yakov's cause finally comes to share what Delmore Schwartz had called " the last alienation." He suffers imprisonment and death for his pains. As Yakov himself remarks towards the end of the novel, Jewish history is like all history only more so. Not only Bibikov, but a number of other non-Jewish characters whose lives brush against his are drawn into the web of his personal fate. There is Kogin the prison-guard who bears witness briefly to Yakov's undeserved torments, and in consequence suffers violent death. And there is the cossack horseman at the end who loses his leg through the explosion of a bomb which a rabid anti-semite had aimed at Yakov as he was being driven through the streets to the courthouse for his trial. The Jewish fate, the Jewish victim psychology is infectious. It involves men of all kinds, including those who are by nature and background unsympathetic to the Jewish cause. By being placed within the spiritual zone of Jewish suffering they become involved.

This is precisely the phenomenon, too, which Malamud exhibits in *The Assistant* (1957) where an Italian born gentile, Frank Alpine, is gradually drawn into the psychic sphere of a Jewish family, that of Morris Bober, a New York grocer who Alpine had earlier robbed and beaten, and whose daughter he had raped. But Alpine changes, and his circumcision at the end symbolizes (again in allegorical fashion) the extension of the Jewish life-pattern to the gentile, now purged of his evil propensities. It also symbolizes the Jew's exposure to, and knowledge of pain almost from the hour of his birth. This environment of pain has now become a universal condition, a characteristic of the American urban wilderness-dweller. There are mythic overtones here (as in Malamud's fiction generally), and Alpine seems to be enacting a kind of ' Quest ' ritual. Through this solemn initiation rite the Wasteland will be redeemed. But it is an ironical redemption, for the Jew, whilst pointing out the path of salvation, never ceases to be a victim.

The special interest of the figure of the Jew in present-day American literature is thus twofold. He is on the one hand the archetypal victim and 'shlemiel': and he is on the other hand the surviving witness to those moral and social virtues enshrined in the Declaration of Independence. The Jew by being more sinned against than sinning becomes, symbolically again, the representative of justice and the rights of man. And here is one of the permanent themes of American literature as a whole. He is Max in Richard Wright's *Native Son*. And Max the champion of law and goodness, the saviour of the human image, belongs to that line of hero-figures which stretches back through Huck Finn and the romantic heroes of James Fenimore Cooper to the Puritan beginnings of the American conscience. In other words, he is pure American. Looked at from the outside, the belief in the humanizing ethical mission of America may seem terribly flawed by hypocrisy, self-deception and worse, but the student of literature will not be carried away by this latter day reaction to American idealism. Flawed as it is, it is impossible to understand the history of the United States and its literature without it. Such idealism is basic to the career of Abraham Lincoln and the founding fathers of the colonies alike. They were spurred on—among other things—by a belief in man as born equal, created in the image of God, and thus somehow capable of saving himself and the world.

Now such moral ideals do not only have a recognizable link with the Hebraic tradition: they are also felt to be linked to it. The Jew tends to be the spokesman of the messianic side of the American social consciousness. The words used by the authors of the American constitution have an unmistakable Biblical echo, and the lines on the Statue of Liberty: " Give me your tired, your poor, your huddled masses yearning to breathe free," were written by a Jewish poetess. It is thus natural that Morris Bober, Yakov Bok and Moses Herzog should continue to witness to the notion of man being—in spite of ugliness, weakness, and defeat—somehow created in the divine image.

The Jew is both saviour and victim, both lost sheep and guide to the perplexed. Through the imagery which the Jew has made available America has been perceived both as a wilderness and a Promised Land. Thus George Washington declared in an epistle to the Jews of Newport in 1790:

> May the Children of the Stock of Abraham, who dwell in this land, continue to merit and enjoy the good will of the other inhabitants: while everyone shall sit in safety under his own vine and figtree, and there shall be none to make him afraid.

If Abraham is, as in Delmore Schwartz's poem, the father of all exiled and alienated humanity, he is also for George Washington the father of those who live out the dream of El Dorado in the promised land.

Here, then, are the two components of the Jewish stereotype as they present themselves in present-day American literature. Yakov Bok, we have said is a victim, a sufferer, but he is also a hero of the faith. His ride to the courthouse at the end of the novel becomes a triumph: he mediates salvation to the huddled masses striving to be free. Of course, he is a saviour of a special kind: it is his Job-like insistence on his own integrity which will lead to the discomfiture of his enemies, not the might of his right arm.

Saul Bellow's hero Moses Herzog (1964) is also saviour and victim combined. But the combination is darker, more harrowing. Herzog is sick, and his sickness is that of the Wasteland, of the urban jungles of New York City and Chicago. He is an outcast in an incoherent world. The family bond has been radically violated: his own promiscuity and his wife's treachery combine to create an environment in which security and happiness for his children are hardly to be thought of. Nor is Moses simply a victim: he is himself contaminated, sunken (to use his own words) in " the creative depth of modern degeneracy."

He is at once victim, scapegoat, and accomplice. He is conscious of the radical collapse of western civilization both around him and within him, his neurosis—for he spends a lot of time with his psychiatrist—being but the symbol of a more universal disease. In Poland he visits the ruins of the Warsaw ghetto, but this becomes part of the general landscape of alienation. It mingles with his own sexual adventures and with the general brutality of mankind in a shrinking world.

But all this is only one side of the picture. Through his moral distortions and aberrations Herzog carries in his soul the memory of a more organic life which somehow lurks behind the present, and the hope of a more blessed future in which everyone shall sit in safety under his own vine and figtree. This part of the American dream is still active in the scenes at Ludeyville, the New England country home where Moses comes to rest at the end of the novel. Somewhere back in the consciousness of the American is the forest, the good land where Indian and White man shall sit together and smoke the pipe of peace. In this sense Moses is not only a professor of romantic literature but a romantic himself. And here his Jewish memories come to his aid. He recalls his childhood in Napoleon Street, Montreal, the childhood of a second generation immigrant:

> Napoleon Street, rotten, toylike, crazy and filthy, riddled, flogged with harsh weather—the bootlegger's boys reciting ancient prayers. To this Moses' heart was attached with great power. *Here was a wider range of human feelings than he had ever again been able to find.* The children of the race, by a never-failing miracle, opened their eyes on one strange world after another, age after age, and uttered the same prayer in each, eagerly loving what they found. What was wrong with Napoleon Street? thought Herzog. All he ever wanted was there.

There is profound irony here. Napoleon Street, as he makes clear, was the scene of poverty, childhood frustrations, petty crime, and unrewarded struggle. But the positive side is clear also. It was a place where the human image, the human dignity had been preserved. There sanctity and humanity still persisted.

He is thus like one of Zangwill's Children of the Ghetto still nourishing in an alien world the Jewish dream of holiness. But what must be insisted upon again is that though the vocabulary of this retrospect is Jewish, the syntax is pure American. What Herzog remembers from his childhood is the good life which (in fact or fantasy) still haunts the American imagination. For Fitzgerald it is the patriarchal society of the Midwest at the beginning of the century: for Faulkner it is the vestigial echo of the patrician order of life in the south: for Bellow it is the Jewish family pattern of the immigrant household that fills him with grief and nostalgia. And like the old-world pattern of the South in Faulkner, or the Midwest in Fitzgerald, Bellow's vision is of a past gone beyond recall. In this he differs from Zangwill, for whom the ghetto continued to be in some sense a viable system. For the latter-day American Jewish novelists this is no longer so. The nightmare is too real for the dream to replace it, so they must accept them both and live in the light of their unmitigated contradictions.

Several critics have pointed out that Herzog is linked by many threads to a great novel of an earlier generation, namely, Joyce's *Ulysses*. Bellow seems to have been using the earlier work as a stylistic model and as a landmark. The name of Bellow's hero, to start with, is taken from Joyce's novel where Moses Herzog a grocer of Dublin is mentioned several times: his personality blends with that of the hero, Bloom. Like Leopold Bloom himself he is the victim of persecution. And here is the link, too, with Bellow's hero who is from the start a victim. Leopold Bloom and Bellow's Moses Herzog are both cuckolds, both victims of treacherous women and overbearing men (the adulterer in each case is a loud man in show business); and both of them in a world of hatred and inhuman self-seeking affirm the value of love. It is the word which

Bloom had injected into the hate-loaded atmosphere of Barney Kiernan's pub, and it is the word which Herzog pronounces in the face of his wife's treachery. " I do love you, Madeleine," he says. Both Bloom and Herzog have their weaknesses, but they share, too, the belief that force, hatred, and insult are the opposite of true life, and that true life for men and women can only be founded on love. It is the only means of safeguarding the human image in an increasingly inhuman world.

We noted in an earlier chapter that Joyce had provided his novel with two heroes, Bloom and Dedalus. Bloom represents the World and the Flesh, whilst Dedalus represents the intellectual principle. But they are also " father " and " son." Leopold has literary ambitions which are fulfilled in Dedalus, whilst Dedalus finds in Bloom a certain human warmth which he is seeking. Their meeting is short-lived : the dark Jew and his fair " offspring," the hoary semite and the young hellenic man of imagination have a certain necessary connexion, but they do not fuse. In Bellow's *Herzog,* however, the hero combines the intellectual and sensual principles in one composite personality. He is both Bloom and Dedalus. The contradictions of the dual image are still there but they have been interiorized within one personality, that of Moses Herzog.

In Herzog's many erotic escapades we sense his submission to the dark gods of the earth, of the flesh. This comes out clearly in his relation with Ramona. She is a priestess of sex. Like Molly Bloom she is Gea-Tellus, a goddess of the earth, and to her deep natural rhythm he submits. But there is the other side to Herzog—the Dedalus side—for he knows also that such submission is failure, and that ultimately his freedom depends on some set of values which shall transcend mere natural instinct :

> her hair in black curls, her face, her mouth painted ; he could smell the perfume. In the depths of a man's being there was something that responded with a quack to such perfume. Quack ! a sexual reflex that has nothing to do

with age or subtlety, wisdom, experience, history, *Wissenschaft, Bildung, Wahrheit.*

Which shall triumph, the all-devouring sex-reflex, or wisdom, experience, and history? The inner struggles of Herzog condense themselves into just this—the attempt to oppose to the deep rhythm of nature, to the downward drag of contemporary culture an affirmation of some higher intellectual principle which shall provide for truth, science, and the life of the spirit, in short a viable future for the human race. Moses it is true, seeks consolation in sex, but it is no less true to say that is struggling (like Joseph in *Dangling Man,* 1944) against a number of powerful female characters who are trying spiritually to castrate him. Here are the two poles of his psychic situation. His problem is to circumscribe (or shall we say, circumcize) the limits of animal nature. Moses has sunk into the abyss of alienation, of degeneration. He has shared the modern primitive reversion with a zeal derived from his Hebraic antecedents, for Paganism takes on an extra force when the spiritual intensities of the Jew comes to its aid. But on the other hand Moses knows a different principle of life too. He is Moses Herzog, the grandson of Rabbi Sandor-Alexander Herzog, and like Moses of old he carries in his hands the tables of the covenant, that same hoary ancient wisdom of the Semite which had drawn Dedalus to Leopold Bloom. It is these contradictions which define the character and dramatic function of Moses Herzog and make of his portrait a peculiarly poignant present-day example of the dual image.

The kind of archetypal myth with which we are here concerned does not require for its presentation a great work of art. It is possible for it to find expression in more ephemeral examples as well. Philip Roth's successful novel, *Portnoy's Complaint* (1967) is really a vulgarized version of *Herzog.* The same kind of story-line is used (possibly in imitation of *Herzog*). There is a sick narrator whose confessions on the psychiatrist's couch form the substance of the novel. There is a slick use of language and some amusing sketches of home life in Newark, New Jersey, but basically the novel exploits in a lurid form those contradictions and paradoxes which better writers have explored in a subtler and richer fashion.

The title of Roth's book is itself ambiguous. Alex Portnoy's ' complaint ' is both a *protest* against society in general and Jewish society in particular, and also a ' complaint ' in the sense of a *disease,* a sickness. That sickness represents the last extreme of degeneration and alienation —alienation in the special sense of a man alienated from himself, and engaged in the abuse of his own mind and body. Roth does not spare us the clinical details of Portnoy's ' complaint.' His hero wallows in self-hatred and disgust. And he makes it clear that his sexual deviations, in particular his insatiable desire for the flesh of gentile women, have developed as a reaction to Judaism and to a claustrophobic Jewish home environment. It is his way of escaping from the burden of belonging to the " Chosen People." It is a biological revolt against the Jewish family, the cornerstone of which is the assumption of responsibility for a future generation which shall continue to carry on the burden of Jewish existence. Instead of fulfilling the destiny marked out for him as ' nice Jewish boy ' who would marry, settle down, and become a credit to his parents in one of the recognized professions, Alex Portnoy spends his time hunting for " shikses " with whom he will indulge in unfruitful and degrading forms of sexuality. In his sexual relations there is nothing left of that unselfish love which still operates as a word of power for Moses Herzog and Leopold Bloom. Portnoy's oedipal love for his mother, itself streaked with hatred, has corrupted all his other relationships until self-hatred only remains. In effect he accuses his mother of having inflicted on him a moral and physical castration.

Portnoy's ' depravities ' hurt himself more than they hurt others. In spite of his fears, he is not likely to end in the police-court; but his behaviour bears an ominous

resemblance to that of the bad Jew in such anti-Semitic
fiction as George du Maurier's *Trilby*. There, too, Svengali's chief enormity is his vile pursuit of the white gentile
woman. So much so that Gershom Scholem has been
prompted to remark that *Portnoy's Complaint* is the book
that the anti-Semites have been trying to write for a
hundred years without succeeding: finally a Jew has succeeded in writing it. But this is not quite true: there is
another half of Portnoy's personality which Scholem has
not weighed in his summing-up. For with considerable
insight Roth displays in his protagonist not only the ' bad
Jew ' of legend, but the residual ' good Jew ' as well. Alex
Portnoy is also the passionate righter of wrongs. His job
in the city for which his moral idealism well fits him is
that of " Assistant Commissioner for the City of New
York Commission on Human Opportunity." The deliberately inflated title indicates the intention to caricature
the moral fixation of the Jew who is heir to the messianic
dream of reform inscribed by Emma Lazarus on the Statue
of Liberty:—" Give me your tired, your poor, your
huddled masses yearning to breathe free." Portnoy devotes
his life—that is to say the overt public portion of his life—
to providing human opportunities for the huddled masses
in the coloured sections of New York, for the poor whites
and the Puerto Ricans. He contemplates this social activity
with a certain grimace of self-conscious irony, but it is
real nevertheless, as real as the obscene language and the
secret indulgences. He is the " high-minded civil liber-
tarian " who as a boy had followed with passionate concern the allied struggle against Nazism in Europe, and
had burned with a desire to plant social justice in America.
Moreover, Roth sees that it is the attractiveness for the
white Anglo-Saxon women of the Jew with the social conscience, the moral zeal, and the sense of family loyalty
which explains the other side of the notorious charge of
Rassenschande. Miscegenation of Jewish man and gentile
maid (the theme also of so much sentimental and non-
sentimental fiction in Zangwill, in Golding, or more re-

cently in Dan Jacobson) is not only to be explained as a ritual expression of the Jew's desire to escape the burden of his own Jewishness, but also as an expression of the gentile woman's desire to acquire for herself and her children " a regular domestic Messiah . . . a Jewish boy just dying in his every cell to be Good, Responsible, and Dutiful to a family of his own." With his messianic fervour and charm, he is for her the antithesis of the mean, drinking and gambling Anglo-Saxon spouse. Here in this dialectical relation of attraction and repulsion between Jew and Gentile is surely part of the interior mechanism of the dual image. The Jew is found attractive for possessing precisely those virtues which come to him from the tradition he is seeking to throw off. In throwing it off he gains freedom, but he also learns to despise himself; and despising himself he cannot help but make himself an object of contempt to his gentile partner also.

The Biological Revolt

The negative inversion of the Jew, his revolt and self-hatred cannot go much further than the point reached in *Portnoy*. And that is because what has now been discarded is that last bastion of Jewish existence in exile, namely, the "yiddishe mama." In Henry Roth's novel *Call It Sleep* the oedipal crisis had caused the child to rise against the Jewish father (or at least to flee from his face) but the mother had been spared. She remained to comfort the child. And if one goes back further one finds that the basic revolt is one of sons against fathers: this is the pattern in Zangwill, in Adele Wiseman, in Peretz and the Jewish writers of the *Haskalah* period in nineteenth century Europe. The father had represented law, history, the responsibilities of the covenant. Behind the Jewish father, stands the Father, that heavenly Father against whom the over-burdened son revolts by throwing off the heavy yoke of the commandments. Thus the Rabbi's son in *Children of the Ghetto* abandons the Ghetto, the Jewish dietary code and the Festivals. But in how many novels of this kind does the Jewish mother not still stand firm clutching her children to her bosom, maintaining a clandestine correspondence with the straying sheep of the flock of Abraham to guard them against the wrath of the enraged father-figure? It is a classic situation. If such revolt against the father included also the motif of intermarriage, that merely represented one final move in the drama of apostasy. The young man remained a Jew and could return to the fold (as he frequently did) and to his mother's apron-strings. The rejection of the "yiddishe mama," however, represents a much more radical break. It marks the final revolt against the biological structure of the Jewish family itself, against Jewish togetherness and identity. Portnoy's father is a marginal figure who merely echoes his wife's hysterical complaints. It is the mother who through her enveloping and smothering presence drives her son into outer darkness. As a consequence he withdraws entirely from Jewish existence. It is a total abdication, for the stream of Jewish history is cut off at the source, at its biological headsprings.

This radical revolt against the Jewish mother has been building up in the mid-twentieth century in Jewish writing on both sides of the Atlantic. In Brian Glanville's *The Bankrupts,* the father, though a vicious personality ever in the background, is by no means so central a figure as the mother against whom the daughter's venom is chiefly directed. In the bitter quarrel at the centre of the book Rosemary calls her mother a bitch, and the ensuing flight of the daughter from the household symbolizes her final break with the Jewish family pattern. Glanville notably employs the imagery of the womb to describe the warm comfortable ambience of the Jewish middle-class home. It is this that Rosemary is rejecting—the actual matrix of the family. In Anglo-Jewish writers less directly concerned with Jewish existence the same tendency to see the Jewish mother as the target is evident. Bernard Kops in *The Dream of Peter Mann* (1960) introduces Sonia, a Jewish mother, bullying, assertive, and trying to monopolize her offspring through the force of an overpowering affection:

> The things I did for you. Everything I sacrificed to make you happy and safe. I won't talk about your father, but you, you were the apple of my eye, etc.

In the end, of course, he breaks free. Kops is not concerned with the break-up of Jewish life as such. The little vignette of Peter and Sonia functions as part of a Brechtian analysis of society and its imminent decay. The play celebrates the break-down of the middle class family code in the apocalyptic era of the atom-bomb.

There is here a salutary footnote to the matters discussed in this chapter. We should beware of giving a specifically Jewish interpretation to the inner conflicts of Portnoy or of the characters of Malamud and Bellow. We are not here concerned (as in Zangwill and Cahan) with the crisis of assimilation. Total assimilation has already been achieved. The characters dealt with are full-blooded Americans. If assimilation is the great fall from grace which occurs in Jewish history, then the events celebrated in these novels occur after the fall. We are no longer concerned with Jewish history as such. Even the oedipal crisis of Portnoy has a wider, a more universal application. It is true that at the centre of the book we behold a Jewish home and a Jewish mother and that this gives a certain extra emotional charge to the drama, but in an age when a radical breakdown of standards, a radical permissiveness threatens the structure of the family generally both in the United States and elsewhere, it is clear that what we have here is a very widespread ' complaint' indeed. The dual image has become a mechanism for articulating the spiritual condition of a large section of mankind. The Peace Corps and hippydom are two sides of one coin. Idealism and moral anarchy flourish side by side in a society which has long ago thrown off the stern father and is now in the process of throwing off the indulgent mother. The exiled Jew is not responsible for this situation, but he can help to interpret it: and it is this which makes him a culture-hero. He has a further contribution to make also: he contributes the sense of guilt. It is true that Bellow and Roth do not offer salvation; they do not offer a cure for the spiritual diseases of their characters; but through the obsessive guilt which moves them to confess their sins, we have at least a testimony to the fact that all is not well, and that a society divided against itself requires healing and salvation.

CHAPTER SEVEN

THE ISRAELI CATHARSIS

The Israeli Catharsis

One of the surprising features of the renaissance of Jewish writing both in England and America in the last twenty years or so is that it has taken place at the same time as that most astonishing of events in modern Jewish history, namely, the rise of the State of Israel, and yet has had little or no reference to it. There is a tremendous new interest in the Jewish home background. Translations of yiddish writers such as Sholom Aleikhem and Isaac Bashevis Singer make best-sellers or, transformed into musicals, become Broadway hits. Hassidic tales and yiddish words are *chic*. Without some yiddish it is said to be almost impossible to gain a footing in New York literary society! But if the Jewish past—in Europe or the lower East Side—has suddenly come to seem full of charm, the Jewish future and the surely not insignificant reality of the Jewish present in the Land of Israel have become strangely charmless.

Moses Herzog mentions Israel as a place that he visits on his eastern tour: he remembers a cool cave in Sodom. But it makes little impact on him; clearly, the centre of his crisis is in America. Even Leopold Bloom's imagination forty years before the rise of Israel had turned more romantically to the east, to the orange groves and melon-fields north of Jaffa, to Jerusalem the Holy City, and to the past glories of Judea. Such imagery is surely a part of the ' Jewish consciousness ' of Bloom, and it operates as a counterpoint to the drabber contents of his imagination giving to his personality a certain exotic flavour. But

Below finds little need of this; and the same is true of Kops, Wesker, Pinter and Malamud, whose major works likewise fail to register the Israeli experience. One simple answer to this would be to say—as we have already said—that these writers are fundamentally American (or British) and that the process of assimilation is for them already complete. Jewish characters, Jewish images, and Jewish reminiscences are only of value to them to the extent that they aid them in articulating the dreams, frustrations, or nightmares associated with American (or British) life. In this context the remembered pieties of Jewish ghetto (or semighetto) existence are relevant. They represent that forgotten good life located just over the rainbow. The new reality of Israel, romantic yes, but also disturbingly unfamiliar to the cultured American or British imagination in its bareness and in the kind of toil and struggle which it imposes, does not fit in in the same way.

All this is partially true, but as an explanation it is not quite satisfactory. The fact is that the rise of Israel *does* make an impact on the American imagination. At a certain level it has a powerful cultic significance. *Exodus* was not only a best-seller but also a highly successful motion picture. The American Jew or gentile has in the past twenty years nourished his imagination on the splendours and trials of a renascent Israel struggling for existence, rising with new-found force to overthrow an enemy more numerous and better equipped than itself. In James Michener's *The Source* (1965) the new-found glory of Israel fuses with past glories to form a tapestry highly accessible to the western imagination with its incurably romantic bent, and its instinctive sympathy for the exercise of power on behalf of a small and brave people. In a way it could be maintained that nothing appeals more to that chivalric imagination, no archetype is more sustaining than the image of power yoked to justice. That is why the cops always win in the gangster films and that is why the good guys are not only saved, but they invariably save themselves with the force of their strong right arm. And the Biblical resonance of the events makes the appeal even stronger. David and Goliath is for America, and for England too, a fundamental metaphor. And that is the manner in which Leon Uris presented the theme of Israel reborn. His success was thus predictable. And Israel's right-hand has not forgotten its cunning. From the Suez War of 1956 through the Six Days' War of 1967 and beyond it has been David and Goliath repeated; and Jew and gentile reading the coloured magazine, or gazing spellbound at the Israeli war films have responded accordingly. Why then have the leading Jewish writers not responded? Why does this theme leave Bellow, Malamud and Wesker cold? We may surmise that it would not have failed to inspire Walter Scott, James Fenimore Cooper, Melville, or Hemingway. Melville would not have written a book as cheaply romantic as *Exodus,* but neither on the other hand would he have sent his hero to Chicago and the evil city blocks there to nurse a sickness unto death when he might have sent him to the harsher scenery of Palestine (where in fact he sends his hero, Clarel) to fight the great white whale and return triumphant. And as for distance, the Israel of 1970 is really no further away from America than the Russian world of 1911 which Malamud exhibits so successfully in *The Fixer.*

If then Bellow and Malamud have left the Israel theme out of their work, it is not because to include it would have been to engage in un-American activities. This is not the case at all. The reason is rather that their assimilation to American culture is a partial and limited assimilation. Fiedler has well said that the Jew represents the *superego* of America : the Negro represents the *id.* If the Jew stands for the moral virtues, the Negro stands for power, violence, the force of the right arm. The two do not combine. A Jewish movement to achieve equal rights for Jews in golf clubs and universities is conceivable, but a Jewish takeover of Columbia in the name of 'Jewish Power' is inconceivable. Yet, that is what has happened in Israel. It is no wonder then that the American Jewish writer—the writer, that is, who really interprets the soul of the assimilated, alienated, bourgeois, latter-day decadent American—has no place in his imagination for Israel. " Violence," says Bellow's Moses Herzog, when he sorrowfully puts back his father's revolver in the desk, "is for the *goy*." He has conveniently forgotten that in Israel, a mere ten hours' flying-time away, violence, exercised in the name of historic right, has become very much a Jewish quality. But then to have taken that into account would have meant becoming something of a Hemingway, a Thomas Wolfe or a James Baldwin. And the Jewish positioning within the pattern of American culture does not permit that kind of acculturation. When Bellow celebrates power (as in *Henderson the Rain King*) it is a mythic power possible only in a fabulous setting: when Malamud gives us an epic hero (in *The Natural*) it is an allegorical or fantastic heroism: when Normal Mailer perversely embraces violence, it becomes a twisted, grotesque, radically diseased violence (as in *The American Dream*). Healthier modes of violence and more natural exhibitions of power are evidently impossible for the Jew, fated as he is to be the spokesman of the American *superego,* its bourgeois conscience. In a more recent novel, *Mr. Sammler's Planet* (1970), Bellow exhibits the same fixation. His hero, an ageing European liberal, looks out of place in the jungle conditions of New York in the late sixties. He notes the callousness of a Negro pickpocket, and later watches with horror as his own son-in-law smashes the Negro's face. He has the memory also of his own aggressions when serving as a partisan in the Polish forests. Violence fascinates him: he had travelled to Israel to watch the fighting in 1967. But he returns to America to be the apostle there of a dying civilization, that of pre-War Bloomsbury. Such is his cultural destiny.

Roth's hang-up in *Portnoy's Complaint* is similar. After plumbing the depths of degradation in a hotel room in Athens, Portnoy beats it to Tel-Aviv. He goes on the tourist circuit; Carmel caves, Bet-Shean excavations, Kibbutzim, and Chagall windows. But he does more than that, he takes stock of the Israeli and realizes how utterly different he is from the American Jewish bourgeois:

> In their short pants the men remind me of the head counselors at the Jewish summer camps I worked at during college vacations—only this isn't summer camp, either. It's home! . . . . These are (there's no other word) the natives. Returned! This is where it all began! Just been away, on a long vacation, that's all! Hey, here we're the WASPs!

He might have added that here we're the Negroes and here we're the Mexicans. But with the small difference that, hard as we try, we cannot quite shed the Hebraic conscience either, the dream of a messianic salvation for mankind. Such a combination of *id* and *superego* is inaccessible in American terms. The Puritan conscience and the endemic violence of America have never truly made peace with one another. Portnoy fails to make it in Israel, both in the emotional and in the sexual sense. The vision of the Jewish renaissance where the Jews are the 'Wasps' renders him impotent; it is outside his range. His oedipal crisis is now complete: in the faces of the Israeli girls with whom he seeks intimacy he sees the face not only of all the gentile women whom he has desired, but also of the mother whom he loves and from whom he must at all costs break free. Them he cannot conquer: they are both too close to him and too far away. So he flees the scene. Ironically, Roth heads the final chapter of his book in which Portnoy gains his Israeli revelation: " In Exile." For him Israel is the exile, and the good advice given him there is, " You should go home." He returns to the familiar city blocks and to his job as Assistant Commissioner for Human Opportunity.

It could be claimed that the Israeli reality is constantly there, a scarcely acknowledged presence in the imagination of the present-day American writer. It is the invisible side of the moon. Perhaps Malamud's *The Fixer* indicates this

—the name of the hero, Yakov Bok, is a giveaway. Jacob-Yakov represents that side of the Jewish historical experience which is the antithesis of Israel-Yisrael. Yakov is the peaceful tent-dweller; his way is that of guile and self-effacement rather than violence. He tries to buy off his brother Esau by gifts and blandishments. He is the home-dweller, the family man; at the same time he is the man of sorrows. Few and evil were the days of the years of his life: this too sums up the life-pattern of Yakov Bok. But Yakov (as Malamud well knows) undergoes an amazing transformation. Left alone for one terrible night he strives with his enemy and prevails, receiving for his reward the name of Israel, signifying triumph and power, God-given strength. This is the transformation that conspicuously does not take place in the life of Yakov Bok. He remains fixed in the character of Jacob, the mild commercial traveller, the Willy Loman of Jewish history. But he is a hero nevertheless. And with great insight Malamud indicates to us that his heroism consists precisely in his avoidance of violence. Violence is for the Goy. He only once, in a weak moment, raises his hand against his persecutors. And by doing so he very nearly brings ruin upon himself. Not for him, and not for the American Jewish writer, the path of armed insurrection, the thunder of the captains and the shouting. His God requires patience and suffering rather than heroic struggle in the cause of a nation reborn. The antithesis between these two images, unacknowledged as it is, represents one other latter-day version of our theme.

The treatment of Israel by Jewish writers in our time has thus tended to be a spasmodic affair eccentric to their main concerns. Sometimes writers have felt that so big a fact as Israel must somehow be included in the pattern, and the result has been frequently artistic failure, or relative failure. In *The Bankrupts* Glanville sends his hero off to Palestine to be killed, and his heroine, Rosemary, follows with their child to become a member of a Kibbutz. It is her way of sealing her revolt against the Jewish family

pattern. The ending of the novel does not carry conviction. In *The Beginners* (1966), a somewhat chaotic novel
by the South African Jewish writer, Dan Jacobson, Israel
is seen as a partial answer to the troubles of a deracinated
Jewish youth growing up amid the political turmoils of
South Africa. But the note of confusion is uppermost.
Vanquish the Angel (1955) by Diana and Meir Gillon,
writers with Israeli affiliations, is a not especially impressive attempt to render the new human and spiritual realities in the land of Israel. In the two chief characters, Yoel
Bar Ze'ev and Olivia Turner, we see a new version
(strangely transported to the Palestine scene) of the sentimental inter-marriage theme with which we have become
familiarized in the writings of Louis Golding and others,
here symbolising the co-operation of the English and
Jewish races in bringing about a Jewish National Home.
Apart from this, its value is chiefly that of a competent
documentary novel describing the situation prior to the
establishment of the Jewish State, and the tensions between
the different communities followed by the period of the
War of Liberation. But there are intimations in the novel
of some new messianic ferment, some vision which must
finally come to complete and sanctify the Jewish physical
and national rebirth:

> There must be something that the genius of the new Israel,
> reunited with its ancient soil, would give, when the time
> was ripe, to the world . . .

We get a firmer realization of the Israeli world in Arthur
Koestler's *Thieves in the Night* (1946), probably the best
novel in English so far to deal with the new reality. Perhaps
this is because Koestler stands outside the Diaspora situation entirely. He does not seem to have any inner Jewish
demon to exorcise, and the result is that he can face the
Israeli situation realistically and positively without the
' Diaspora complexes ' of a Malamud or a Bellow. What
Koestler discerns (both in *Thieves in the Night* and his
later book on Israel, *Promise and Fulfilment*, 1952) is a

human situation still marked by duality and paradox. He praises the courage of the new fighters and settlers but smiles at what he feels is the absurdity of their brand of religious mysticism and the quixoticism of their practical socialism. Past and present have not (for him) convincingly joined hands: romance and realism have not been made one.

The best Israeli writers too are aware of the fact that spiritual discords are still present in their environment. The dual image is a major theme of Israeli life and literature also—the ' old ' Jew and the ' new ' Israeli confronting each other across a gulf of hostility and misunderstanding. The Jew of tradition looks like a bad, weak-kneed specimen in the eyes of the new tough Jew; whilst in the eyes of the pious who have brought to Israel their synagogues and talmudical academies, the new, hard-boiled Jew seems to be frighteningly deficient in the moral and spiritual virtues. The tongue may be that of Jacob, but the hands are those of Esau. And yet there is also a feeling —and it is deep on both sides—that Israel is really on the road to coherence, to a new union of opposites. In fact, it is this very feeling that gives meaning and content to Zionism: it is its ultimate motive force. For why else has the Jew returned to his ancestral land if not to resolve his ambiguities? It he cannot achieve integration there, and peace to his spirit, where else will he achieve them?

The poets may have the last word. They will often see further and deeper than the novelists, seeing unity in place of discord. Thus Karl Shapiro testifies to the revolutionary change in the affairs of the Jewish people, in its *spiritual* posture, which the rise of Israel signifies: the fences, he says, crumble in his flesh:

> When I see the name of Israel high in print
> The fences crumble in my flesh ; I sink
> Deep in a Western chair and rest my soul.
> I look the stranger clear to the blue depths
> Of his unclouded eye. I say my name
> Aloud for the first time unconsciously.

> Speak of the tillage of a million heads
> No more. Speak of the evil myth no more
> Of one who harried Jesus on his way
> Saying, *Go faster*. Speak no more
> Of the yellow badge, *secta nefaria*.
> Speak the name only of the living land.
> *(Poems of a Jew)*

The evil myth is gone, but Shapiro cannot easily define what has taken its place except a new-found self respect which he unconsciously feels even as he remains " chained in a Western chair." Abraham M. Klein, the Canadian Jewish poet, is more explicit. He gazes upon the amazing contradictions of Jewish history and sees them blending and dissolving into some new vision of purposive unity. He sees the new Jew as fully born, a whole man in whom the past and present vitally cohere. It is a daring imaginative leap taking him beyond the present with its problems and disappointments. Klein's Biblical imagery is notable, and his verse has a Blakeian freedom:

> O who is this, rising from the Sharon, bearing a basket of grapes, vaunting the golden apples? And who is he, that other one, following behind a plough, breaking the soil, as hard as the heart of Pharaoh?
>
> If this be a Jew, indeed, where is the crook of his spine; and the quiver of lip, where?
>
> Behold his knees are not callous through kneeling; he is proud, he is erect.
>
> There is in his eyes no fear, in his mind no memory of faggots.
>
> And these are not words wherewith one tells a Jew.
>
> Truly this is such a one; he has left his hump in Ashkinaz; in Sphorad his maimed limb; beyond the seas his terror he has abandoned.
>
> He has said to the sun, Thou art my father that gives me strength; and to the cloud, Thou art my mother suckling me thy milk.

The sign of his father is on his brow, and the breath of his mother renders him fragrant. No legion affrights him, no flame in the dark, no sword in the sun. For a thousand shall come upon him, and a thousand be carried away.

A son has returned to her that bore him; at her hearth he grows comely; he is goodly to behold.

Behind the bony cage where beats the bird of joy; within the golden cup is wine that overflows.

(*Hath Not a Jew*, 1940)

Klein's most considerable work, *The Second Scroll* (1951) goes deep into the heart of Jewish experience in the years following the Holocaust and the rise of Israel. It moves between the poles of triumph and anguish. It is these that have to be brought into focus in order that the Jew should become an integrated moral being. Thus Klein embraces in his vision of the new Jew the characters of Jacob and Israel—the shuffling self-effacing victim and the warrior who wrestles with God and prevails. Part novel, part poem, part memoir, *The Second Scroll* presents a journey from Montreal to Safed with stopovers in Rome and Casablanca. Within this frame he brings together the whole extraordinary history of Jewry in the mid-century. It has both a public and a private dimension, for while it springs directly out of the historical situation of an entire people, it is at the same time a personal lament for the members of the poet's family burnt in the crematoria of Auschwitz (" my sundered cindered kin "). He ends with a solemn annunciation which is both psalm and prayer:

Hear me who stand
Circled and winged in vortex of my kin:
Forego the complete doom! The winnowed, spare!
Annul the scattering and end! And end
Our habitats on water and on air!
Gather the flames up to light orient
Over the land; and that funest eclipse,
Diaspora dark, revolve from off our ways.

Towered Jerusalem and Jacob's tent
Set up again ; again renew our days
As when near Carmel's mount we harbored ships,
And went and came, and knew our home: and song
From all the vineyards raised its sweet degrees,
And thou didst visit us, didst shield from wrong,
And all our sorrows salve with prophecies ;
Again renew them as they were of old,
And for all time cancel that ashen orbit
In which our days, our hopes, and kin, are rolled.

For Klein Israel has become the central reality. In that land it may be possible for the Jew to emerge both in literature and in life as a man capable of tenacity, and also of joy, music, song, and the good life. There it may be possible finally to harmonize the portrait of the Jew, to strip him of myth and fantasy, whilst at the same time giving to the demon that possesses him the status of historical fulfilment.

SELECT BIBLIOGRAPHY

(Secondary Sources)

ANDERSON, GEORGE K.
    The legend of the Wandering Jew. Providence, Brown
    University Press, 1965.

CALISCH, EDWARD N.
    The Jew in English literature, as author and as subject.
    Richmond, Bell Book and Stationery Co., 1909.

CHAMBERS, EDMUND K.
    The medieval stage. London, Oxford University Press, 1903.
    2v.

COLEMAN, EDWARD D.
    The Jew in English drama (1943), with a prefatory essay by
    Edgar Rosenberg: The Jew in western drama (1968).
    New York, The New York Public Library, and Ktav, 1970.

FIEDLER, LESLIE A.
    The Jew in the American novel. New York, Herzl Press,
    1959.

FIEDLER, LESLIE A.
    No! in thunder; essays on myth and literature. Boston,
    Beacon Press, 1960.

FISCH, HAROLD.
    Jerusalem and Albion; the Hebraic factor in seventeenth-
    century literature. London, Routledge, 1964; New York,
    Schocken Books, 1964.

FREUND, MARGIT.
    Israel Zangwill Stellung zum Judentum, Berlin, 1927.

KOHUT, GEORGE A.
    A Hebrew anthology. Cincinnati, Bacharach, 1913. 2v.

LANDA, MYER J.
    The Jew in drama. 2nd. ed., introduced by Murray Roston.
    New York, Ktav, 1969.

LEHMANN, RUTH P.
    Nova bibliotheca anglo-judaica. London, Jewish Historical
    Society of England, 1961. Updates Roth's work.

LIPTZIN, SOLOMON.
    The Jew in American literature. New York, Bloch, 1966.

MALIN IRVING.
    Jews and Americans. Carbondale, Southern Illinois Univer-
    sity Press, 1965.

MICHELSON, HIJMAN.
The Jew in early English literature. Amsterdam, Paris, 1926.

MODDER, MONTAGU F.
The Jew in the literature of England to the end of the nineteenth century. Philadelphia, Jewish Publication Society of America, 1939.

NEWMAN, LOUIS I.
Richard Cumberland, critic, and friend of the Jews. New York, Bloch, 1919.

PHILIPSON, DAVID.
The Jew in English fiction. New, rev. & enl. ed. Cincinnati, Clarke, 1911.

ROSENBERG, EDGAR.
From Shylock to Svengali; Jewish stereotypes in English fiction. Stanford, Calif., Stanford University Press, 1960.

ROSTON, MURRAY.
Biblical drama in England from the Middle Ages to the present day. London, Faber, 1968.

ROTH, CECIL.
Benjamin Disraeli, Earl of Beaconsfield. New York, Philosophical Library, 1952.

ROTH, CECIL.
Magna bibliotheca anglo-judaica. New ed., rev. and enl. London, Jewish Historical Society of England, 1937.

SCHULZ, MAX F.
Radical sophistication: studies in contemporary Jewish American Novelists. Athens, Ohio University Press, 1969.

SCHWARCZ, LEO W.
Mutations of Jewish values in contemporary American fiction. Syracuse, New York, 1966.

SINGER, SIMEON.
Literary remains, edited by Israel Abrahams. London, 1908. 3v.

SINSHEIMER, HERMANN.
Shylock, the history of a character. London, Gollancz, 1947.

SOKOLOW, NAHUM.
Hibbath Zion (The love for Zion). Ludwig Mayer, Jerusalem, 1934. On Disraeli, George Eliot and Emma Lazarus.

Trachtenberg, Joshua.
  The devil and the Jews. New Haven, Yale University Press, 1943.

Veen, Harm R. S. van der.
  Jewish characters in eighteenth century English fiction and drama. Groningen, Wolters, 1935.

Wohlgelernter, Maurice.
  Israel Zangwill; a study. New York, Columbia University Press, 1964.

Young, Karl.
  The drama of the medieval church. Oxford, Clarendon Press, 1933. 2v.

THE DUAL IMAGE

INDEX